STUDY SKILLS IN
EDUCATION

Success With
Your Education
Research
Project

STUDY SKILLS IN
EDUCATION

Success With Your Education Research Project

John G. Sharp

For Isobel

First published in 2009 by Learning Matters Ltd.

British Library Cataloguing in Publication Data
A CIP record for this book is available from the British Library.

ISBN: 978 1 84445 133 3

Cover and text design by Toucan Design
Project management by Swales & Willis Ltd, Exeter, Devon
Typeset by Kelly Gray
Printed and bound in Great Britain by TJ International Ltd, Padstow, Cornwall

Learning Matters Ltd
33 Southernhay East
Exeter EX1 1NX
Tel: 01392 215560
info@learningmatters.co.uk
www.learningmatters.co.uk

Contents

About this book

There are many books available which provide an introduction to educational research as well as how to carry out an individual research project but these have generally been written for existing teachers or those setting out to do full-time M-level degrees or PhDs. Surprisingly few introductory texts have ever been written specifically for those studying education or training to be a teacher for the first time. This book is therefore aimed at you if you are enrolled on any of the following.

- An undergraduate or postgraduate course of Initial Teacher Training leading to the award of QTS (primary or secondary).

- A degree in Education or Education Studies with or without QTS.

- A degree in Early Years or Early Childhood Education.

- A foundation degree in education or any education-related subject discipline.

Undertaking some form of small-scale, individual research project is a normal requirement of most undergraduate or postgraduate education courses, one often firmly rooted in personal interest and professional experience. It may turn out to be classroom-based and attached to a placement (e.g. in a school, an outdoor centre, a museum or a gallery) or it may be part of something more traditional and library-based. But how do you get started? You might be lucky enough to get some formal research methods input. But even if you do, the likelihood is that it may not be as directly relevant to your own project as you would like it to be. You might be assigned a supervisor to help. But even if you are, the amount of time your supervisor has for this purpose might be limited to a few short tutorials. Whatever your own course provides, one thing is certain. You'll always need additional support. This book is therefore intended to provide the practical framework around which your own individual research project can be tackled with confidence and completed successfully. Several features are included to help.

- Clearly specified learning outcomes for each chapter.

- Carefully selected and organised text written and presented in a straightforward, no nonsense way.

- Worked examples based upon 'real' projects and 'real' data illustrating and exemplifying different elements of the research process.

- Practical and reflective tasks making full use of the research literature to help develop knowledge and understanding.

- Key points reminding you of what to do and what to avoid.

- Further reading for digging a little deeper.

While there is undoubtedly a wide range of education courses available, with an equally wide range of individual research project requirements and expectations, the practical guidance offered here should be sufficient to draw you into the world of educational research from whichever level you are starting from. By using this book carefully, you will begin to acquire the necessary range of intellectual, practical and transferable skills to lead you towards producing work of the highest possible standard whether in the first, final or only year of study. As is the nature of educational research, of course, nothing which appears in this book is uncontested. The secret is to know when enough is enough and move on.

Further reading

If at any time you find the need to consult more widely or perhaps would like an alternative perspective, try these five titles for starters. Bell (2005) is perhaps the most accessible. Cohen et al. (2007) has it all but might be hard work.

Bell, J. (2005) *Doing your research project: a guide for first-time researchers in education, health and social science*. Maidenhead: Open University Press.

Burton, N., Brundrett, M. and Jones, M. (2008) *Doing your education research project*. London: Sage.

Cohen, L., Manion, L. and Morrison, K. (2007) *Research methods in education*. London: Routledge.

Hopkins, D. (2002) *A teacher's guide to classroom research*. Buckingham: Open University Press.

Opie, C. (ed) (2004) *Doing educational research: a guide to first time researchers*. London: Sage.

1. Let's get acquainted

Learning outcomes

Undertaking an individual research project in education can be a particularly daunting task but it really doesn't have to be that way. Once you've tackled some of the ideas and principles underpinning educational research as a whole, the rest, as they say, should be a walk in the park. By having read this chapter and completed the tasks within it, you will:

- know about educational research as a process of enquiry;

- be familiar with the scope of educational research and how it has diversified and become more complex over time;

- be aware of some of the philosophical perspectives associated with educational research in terms of its two major research paradigms;

- be able to identify and evaluate some of the educational research literature available to you in your own library and online.

What is educational research?

Educational research has now become so diverse and complex that beyond even the most basic of definitions it no longer has any single identity. Educational researchers do what they do in a whole manner of different ways, for a whole manner of different reasons and for a whole manner of different purposes. Over the years, the boundaries between the different approaches that exist, the different methods available for collecting data, the different means of data analysis employed and the different philosophical perspectives which bind educational researchers together and shape their values and beliefs have become blurred and confused. As a direct consequence, and while studying education or training to be a teacher for the first time, attempting to understand and to undertake educational research can be a difficult and, at times, hazardous activity. Nevertheless, each and every aspect of your own individual research project has to be justified in full and it is important to be able to attempt to do this well even if it means having to learn to tread delicately through the educational research minefield.

Practical task

The diversity and complexity of educational research

One of the easiest ways to get familiar with the diversity and complexity of research activity within education is to visit the education section of your library. Begin by finding where the current journals are on display. Just take a look at how many different journals exist. Some are very academic in nature while some are very professional. Some publish articles on a wide range of topics while some are very highly specialised. Take a closer look at an academic and professional journal from the area of education you are specialising in or interested in. Compare each one in terms of:

- content;

- writing style;

- accessibility of material;

- presentation.

Which do you prefer and why? Most journals are available online. Find out which e-journals your library subscribes to and how to access them.

Similarly, you can find out about research funded or commissioned by a wide range of educational organisations. In the first instance, a useful shortlist might include:

- the Department for Children, Schools and Families (www.dcsf.gov.uk);

- the Training and Development Agency for Schools (www.tda.gov.uk);

- the Qualifications and Curriculum Authority (www.qca.org.uk);

- the National Foundation for Educational Research (www.nfer.ac.uk).

Visit their websites and browse the research pages. It might also be useful to consult the websites and research pages of the professional associations related to the area of education you are specialising in or interested in too. How do funded or commissioned research reports compare with what you find in journals (content, writing style, accessibility of material, presentation)? Does this tell you anything about the nature of the research and its intended readership?

To get a good feel for how educational research has moved on over the years, find the library shelf holding the books on educational research methods. Try to find one book written in the 1960s, one in the 1980s and one written since 2000. Examine the contents lists in detail. What has changed and what has remained the same? Many books are available online. Find out which e-books your library subscribes to and how to access them.

Towards a definition

In its loosest sense, research concerns itself with finding things out. It follows, then, that educational research can be loosely defined as concerning itself with finding things out about education. Education itself is often presented as something which refers to those morally acceptable activities, formally planned or otherwise, which bring about worthwhile learning. Educational activities do not take place within a vacuum, of course. They are shrouded in most instances by entire education systems such as those which support and govern the day-to-day and longer-term functioning of schools and other educational environments including the likes of outdoor centres, museums and galleries. Each system has its own historical, social and political background and other cultural influences, all of which helps to explain why educational research is as diverse and complex as it is.

So, educational research is something which concerns itself with finding things out about education. This includes everything from the raising and testing of educational theories and hypotheses to undertaking the sorts of investigations which inform educational actions, judgements and debate. It may be pure or applied. But this doesn't really help you here. What you need is an operational definition from which you can begin to visualise the form your own individual research project might take. One particularly extended definition derived from the educational research literature perhaps encapsulates the *essence* of educational research more than any other:

> *Educational research involves the rigorous and ethically appropriate process of arriving at dependable answers to questions and solutions to problems of an educational nature through the systematic collection and critical analysis, interpretation and presentation of relevant data and other forms of information.*

Educational research, then, is something of a process of enquiry with a purpose. In terms of your own individual research project, the purpose might be to obtain empirical evidence with which you can generate valid and reliable educational knowledge in any or all of its many and varied forms, including knowledge for its own sake (knowing *that* . . .), the knowledge to improve practice (knowing *how* . . .) and the knowledge to challenge ways of *looking at* and *seeing* things (knowing *why* . . .). It is equally possible to do all of these things without looking for empirical evidence, of course, but this will be our starting point and theme throughout. As a process of enquiry more often than not involving you and other people (e.g. children, teachers, parents, members of the general public), educational research also involves being reflexive or self-critical. This is important at all times but particularly so when you find yourself placed in a position to influence the research process itself and the findings which emerge from it. In some instances, for example, you may have no choice but to become an active player and voice in your own research project and this must be carefully accounted for in order to eliminate any suggestion that your work might be biased. Whether or not it is possible to ever truly understand or reflect anything of the educational community you aspire to belong to without being a part of it is of fundamental significance.

Practical task

Words and meanings

It's easy when you read a chapter in any book to forget to stop and take stock of what is being said. Education has been described here and elsewhere as best thought of as something which refers to those morally acceptable activities, formally planned or otherwise, which bring about worthwhile learning. What does the term *education* mean to you? What does it mean to have 'received a good education' or to *be educated*? Is the description of education described here acceptable to you or not?

The extended definition of educational research also presented here is both long and loaded. Consider each of the key elements from within the definition in turn and consider what it means:

- rigour;
- ethical;
- process;
- dependable;
- systematic;
- critical;
- analysis;
- interpretation;
- presentation;
- data;
- information.

Are you sure you grasp the full *essence* of educational research from the definition? Are there any other key elements of educational research missing from the definition that you could add? Can you come up with a better definition yourself?

A philosophical diversion

From the extended definition of educational research presented earlier, you might easily be misled into believing that educational research involves experimentation. Certainly, and in the early days of educational research, experiments employing a scientific method of investigation were particularly common. Indeed, many authors have since written about and defended their view that research of an experimental and scientific nature is perhaps the only means for *settling educational disputes* and the only way to avoid throwing out what is known to work well in favour of *inferior novelties.* But the experiment is only one approach among many and experimentation in education today tends to have a more restricted and specialised application. It's just not always appropriate and it doesn't always give you the answers or solutions you need.

Experiments in education, at least those involving a scientific method of investigation, help to exemplify what is referred to in education as the normative research paradigm (also referred to as the positivist or quantitative research paradigm depending on which book you read). This stands in direct contrast to the interpretive research paradigm (also referred to as the anti-positivist or qualitative research paradigm depending on which book you read). Research paradigms in education, the very mention of which takes you into a philosophical arena best avoided where possible, have been usefully described as the networks of coherent ideas about the very nature and existence of the educational world and how these networks and ideas implicitly or explicitly influence the thoughts and actions of researchers who knowingly or unknowingly subscribe to or support them. It's all a bit tricky to the initiated never mind the uninitiated. Research paradigms can, however, provide researchers with a shared sense of purpose in terms of what counts as valid and reliable knowledge and which means of obtaining it are both reasonable and legitimate. From a normative perspective, as it is frequently presented, there exists an educational world entirely independent of the researcher. Its fundamental components, characteristics and the realities that exist within it can be predicted, isolated, measured, tested, quantified and presented objectively. If it helps:

> *Research from a normative perspective can be thought of as something which is very often carried out* on *people, on* places *and on* events *by* looking in *from the outside.*

However, such an impersonal view of the educational world and how it can be investigated is not to everyone's taste. From an interpretive perspective, as it is frequently presented, people themselves are an integral component of their educational world, interacting naturally with it and constantly altering and modifying its characteristics and creating their own realities such that everything evolves continually. If it helps again:

> *Research from an interpretive perspective can be thought of as something which is very often carried out* with *people, in* places, *creating* events *from within.*

Both differ fundamentally in their epistemological and ontological roots. Epistemology, which considers the very nature of educational knowledge itself (e.g. *What counts as educational knowledge and how is it obtained?*), and ontology, which considers the very nature of educational reality (e.g. *What is it possible to know about and how might what is known about be perceived differently?*), are particularly important though needless to say you've probably given very little thought to any of this until now and probably wish it hadn't been brought to your attention at all. Such depictions of the normative and interpretive paradigms in education are, to say the least, unhelpful, however, for they both caricature each perspective to the extreme. What really matters is that you are aware that not everyone will necessarily agree with you about which forms of knowledge and how they are obtained are more valid and reliable than others or *look at* or *see* things the way that you do. Whichever position you subscribe to and whatever form your individual research project takes you must, however, ensure that the approach, methods and means of analysis you employ are *fit-for-purpose.*

Practical task

Identifying your own research perspectives

By now, you will hopefully be thinking about the nature of educational research alongside what you have in mind for your own individual research project. Some of the ideas presented in this chapter will be new to you and perhaps confusing. You won't be the only one confused. Use the following statements to help begin to identify where you sit on the normative-interpretive continuum. Simply place a cross anywhere on the arrowed lines between each pair of statements as guided by the strength of your own feelings. Finish by drawing a single line through each cross to obtain a profile of your own research perspective.

Educational research:

should be objective	←——————→	should be subjective
should provide answers	←——————→	should raise questions
should deal with numbers	←——————→	should deal with words
should be impersonal	←——————→	should be personal
should generalise from findings	←——————→	should interpret specifics
should be detached	←——————→	should be involved
should be realistic	←——————→	should be idealistic
should test hypotheses	←——————→	should generate theories
should find universal truths	←——————→	should find contextualised truths
should be analytical	←——————→	should be descriptive

Does your profile appear to lean more towards the left (i.e. more normative), to the right (i.e. more interpretive) or does it appear more mixed? How is your profile similar to or different from the profiles of others? Discuss the similarities and differences and the possible reasons which might account for them. Are they rooted in educational background, subject specialism, personal experience or some other factors? Do you think your research perspective will have any bearing on your choice of individual research project or how you might go about tackling it?

The paradigm wars

Largely because it came first, some hardened critics wasted little time on deconstructing and attempting to *rubbish* normative research (or at least experimentation employing a scientific method of investigation) in favour of their own preferred alternative. Needless to say, those on the receiving end gave back as good as they got and interpretive research was equally *rubbished* for being methodologically flawed and lacking in rigour. Arguments on both sides varied enormously but often centred on the shortcomings of both normative and interpretive research to bring about educational improvement particularly in schools:

- by generally failing to provide a sound evidence-base for teaching and learning, the raising of educational attainment, informing curriculum development or for the making of policy;

- by generally failing to communicate relevant findings in a manner accessible to teachers, other educators and the general public.

Such a narrow focus, however, only served to distort the scope and purpose of educational research itself and ultimately provided central government with the ammunition it needed in order to perhaps undermine the relevance and independence of educational research as a whole in its drive towards continued educational reform, at least in England and in Wales (e.g. you might like to give some thought to where the motivation for a National Curriculum of subjects actually came from in the first instance or why, if on a course of Initial Teacher Training, you are being trained to teach what you have to teach the way you are). Fortunately, many enlightened educational researchers view both paradigms and the sorts of research and research findings they generate as complementary rather than competing and are happy to shift emphasis towards one or the other as determined by need. It really all boils down to the nature of the questions you ask, the problems you wish to solve and finding the most appropriate ways of sorting it all out.

Reflective task

Competing or complementary?

If you are the kind of person that believes everything on television or in the newspapers then you are probably the kind of person that believes that *all* boys underachieve relative to *all* girls at school and that if you happen to be working class and black then the future is particularly bleak. If you are the kind of person that questions what you encounter then you are probably the kind of person that would find all of this very hard to believe. But surely the evidence speaks for itself? In education and educational research nothing is ever that simple! The articles you are directed to here exemplify how research essentially tackling the same issue but undertaken from very different philosophical perspectives is essential:

- Connolly, P. (2006) Summary statistics, educational achievement gaps and the ecological fallacy. *Oxford Review of Education*, 32(2): 235–252.

- Demie, F. (2005) Achievement of Black Caribbean pupils: good practice in Lambeth schools. *British Educational Research Journal*, 31(4): 481–508.

Connolly argues convincingly that the 'uncritical use' of summary statistics 'encourages the labelling of whole groups of pupils as underachievers or overachievers' the 'adverse consequences' of which result in false gender and ethnic stereotypes and a distortion in the presentation of certain 'educational inequalities'. Demie argues convincingly from case studies that, under the right conditions and circumstances, Black Caribbean pupils can 'buck the national trend [of underachievement] against all odds'. Both authors share a common view that the perception of particularly underachievement based on gender and ethnicity is not only misleading but may have resulted in the misdirection of resources aimed at addressing the issue. Both articles flag up the importance of sensitive educational research informing policy at the highest level.

- Obtain a copy of both articles (online or print) and read each one very carefully.

- Identify the main characteristics which help you to determine which author has adopted a more normative or more interpretive perspective.

- Prepare a summary of each article outlining what the main issues raised are and what evidence is used to support the various positions presented.

- Consider to what extent the research presented is competing or complementary.

Education is a publicly and politically charged arena. Why do you think journalists and politicians continue to misinterpret and misreport the research freely available to them and continue to perpetuate the educational myths that they do? Would you agree or not that tackling the big questions and problems in education requires the integration of educational research perspectives and not a war between them?

In more recent years, and as a result of the paradigm wars, understanding more fully the very nature of educational practice in the classroom-based environments particularly of schools is now a research priority for many. This has brought teachers themselves very much into the research fold, working individually or alongside more research experienced colleagues to address the very real questions and problems that impact upon their everyday lives. As a result, the 'knowledge-for-action' required at the 'chalk-face' is now more readily available than at any time in the past. The emergence of action or practitioner researcher, with an emphasis on self-reflective and evidence-based enquiry, has proved liberating, providing teachers with a facility to make informed decisions for themselves and for others.

Thinking ahead

By now you might be wondering where your own individual research project fits into all of this. The small-scale educational research of the sort you are most likely to undertake while studying education or training to be a teacher for the first time may turn out to be entirely empirical in nature with data collection centre-stage. It is certainly not impossible that you may find yourself working as an action or practitioner researcher of sorts and helping to answer a question or to solve a problem which will impact directly on those around you. You may even find yourself making a very real contribution to how national policy is being implemented in the classroom you find yourself attached to, be it in a school, an outdoor centre, a museum or a gallery. You might just as equally find yourself doing other things entirely including spending long hours in a library sifting through a collection of documents. It'll all depend upon what you choose to do and how you choose to go about doing it or what your own course requirements demand. What is certain is that you will need a great deal of perseverance, flexibility, creativity and patience to succeed, for things never quite go as expected or turn out as you would hope. Eventually, you will be required to make some decisions about which approach, which method and which means of analysis to use but reading the chapters which follow will help. All you have to do now is find a focus, formulate a plan and press ahead. What could be easier!

Summary of key points

Getting started in educational research is sometimes not easy, but with a little bit of effort it's not impossible either.

With educational research, your library really is your best friend. Get to know it well and the resources available to you.

Use the extended definition of educational research presented here to help ensure that your work really is research and not something else entirely.

Research paradigms are important and you should be aware of their influence both personally and within the educational research community as a whole. But unless you are writing about the philosophy of educational research it wouldn't do any harm to give them a miss. The questions you ask and the problems you choose to solve will draw you almost naturally into selecting the best tools for the job (e.g. approach, method and means of analysis).

No particular approach, method or means of analysis has a monopoly on quality and none can deliver outcomes with certainty.

Anybody can do educational research particularly if they seek out and take advice.

Further reading

Bassey (1995) is a classic text which provides a valuable and highly readable introduction to educational research as a whole. Pring (2000) provides an exceptionally clear account of the philosophy of education and educational research including an insight into the paradigm wars. If the history and contested nature of educational research is what you are after, start with Oanacea (2005) and Whitty (2006). Both adopt a meaty documentary analysis (which is useful in itself) and both provide up-to-date reference lists for you to trawl back through.

Bassey, M. (1995) *Creating education through research: a global perspective for the 21st Century*. Newark: Kirklington Moor.

Oancea, A. (2005) Criticisms of educational research: key topics and levels of analysis. *British Educational Research Journal*, 31(2): 157–183.

Pring, R. (2000) *Philosophy of educational research*. London: Continuum.

Whitty, G. (2006) Education(al) research and education policy making: is conflict inevitable? *British Educational Research Journal*, 32(2): 159–176.

2 Finding a focus and formulating a plan

Learning outcomes

As you get down to starting your individual research project, the likelihood is you'll be trying to do lots of different things all at the same time. Finding a focus and formulating a plan as early as possible will help structure your work, keep you on track and identify where the potential pitfalls and hazards lie along the way. By having read this chapter and completed the tasks within it, you will:

- know about research topics, working titles and preliminary research questions;

- be familiar with how to write and develop a research proposal;

- be able to adopt appropriate strategies to organise and manage your time;

- have carefully considered the importance and relevance of research ethics.

So where do the topics for individual research projects come from?

The topic you select and how you approach investigating it define the individual research project giving it both focus and direction. Unless your own course requirements place restrictions on what you can and cannot do, the sky really is the limit. This is what makes the individual research project so exciting and challenging, both for you, your supervisor and any others who might have an interest in your work. Your initial thoughts and ideas concerning topics may be influenced by several factors.

- Something you've read yourself or already encountered as part of your own course.

- Working closely with children and teachers in schools or educators in some other educational environment (e.g. an outdoor centre, a museum or a gallery).

- Working with parents or members of the general public.

- Experiencing teaching, learning and assessment in your own specialist curriculum area or another area of interest.

- Tackling a particular aspect of organisation and management.

- Trialling the use of new educational practices or resources.

Alternatively, you may have other thoughts and ideas of your own, perhaps even on something quite unique. A lot may depend upon whether or not your individual research project is classroom-based and attached to a placement or library-based. Ultimately, of course, the responsibility for everything rests entirely with you. This is why it's an *individual* research project. You are required to work pretty much independently as far as possible with only a little guidance and support from your supervisor. At the end of the day, your individual research project will demonstrate something of your 'research potential' as an emerging member of your chosen academic or professional community. Your individual research project might also be instrumental in helping you secure your first appointment, so take care to give that some consideration too. This can make it all a bit scary and perhaps overwhelming. Feeling scared and overwhelmed from time to time is perfectly normal and everyone will experience some form of project anxiety whether they care to admit it openly or not.

What matters right from the outset is that you brainstorm on paper all of your thoughts and ideas about which topics interest you the most and then select and begin to tease out the one topic emerging as a front runner in more detail as part of a topic web or as a concept map. Once you've started in this way, you can get to digging around in the research literature for anything which matches that topic closely or at a distance. Sometimes just digging around in the research literature provides the topic in the first place. Whichever way, keep a record of what you find for there is really nothing more tedious than having to retrieve articles, books and the like at a later date. Even at this early stage, you may be able to identify whether your topic has a sufficient variety of literature to support it or not. Other easy to identify inhibiting factors may also crop up early too. Discuss what you are looking to do with others on your course. They can sometimes throw in things you'd never ever think of. If anything looks insurmountable, give up and move on. Be clinical about this for not to do so will only waste time. It's all part of the research process.

Practical task

Settling on a topic

As you start out with your own individual research project, take some time to carry out the following.

- Brainstorm your thoughts and ideas about the things that interest you most about teaching or education in general.

- Join up those areas of your brainstormed scribbles and doodles which appeal the most with arrows to produce a more detailed topic web.

- As a single topic emerges, prepare a concept map linking everything together more meaningfully.

Brainstorming is a valuable memory jogging technique which allows you to get everything you can think of out without having to worry about how it all fits together. Topic webs narrow down and begin to structure your thoughts and ideas. Concept maps have the added advantage of linking everything together in a more meaningful way by showing how the different elements of your thinking are related to each other. These three steps should be enough to provide you with something of a potential research route and guide you effortlessly into developing a working title. At the same time, informing your thoughts and ideas by tracking down and reading as much research literature as you can will begin to guide you into thinking about research questions and particular methods of data collection and analysis. There is no substitute for hard graft at this stage but the effort put in now will pay off later.

If you're lucky, you may find an existing study close enough to your initial thoughts and ideas that you could replicate or adjust to fit. Replication is an interesting notion for an individual research project, one which doesn't necessarily mean that you will inevitably plagiarise the work of others. Discuss the pros and cons of replication with your supervisor and find out if such an approach is acceptable. Similarly, your own library may keep copies of previous individual research projects. If you have ready access to these it doesn't do any harm to take a look. But remember, regulations, guidance and marking or grading criteria change and you may have nothing other than an intuitive sense as to whether or not what you are looking at is an example of something outstanding or something that failed.

To be or not to be . . .

As your work takes shape, you should be thinking about giving it a working title. The key term here is 'working'. The likelihood is that the title of your individual research project will change and become more refined the more you read, better reflecting just exactly what it is you are attempting to do. It's quite common to develop the focus of your individual research project from a topic with a working title into the form of a provisional research question. The key term here is 'provisional' as once again the likelihood is that this question will change and become more refined too. The transition from focusing interest on one topic, to a working title to a research question is seamless for some, troublesome for others, but you will get there eventually.

Raising a research question no matter how provisional allows for a more exploratory rather than confirmatory form of investigation that might sit more comfortably with experimentation and hypothesis testing. That said, it should be clear and ultimately researchable. Expressed well, a good research question will also stop you from making the big mistake of setting out to prove what you suspect or believe to be true or reinforcing your own values and beliefs. Always retain an open mind. There is some debate about whether or not one research question is ever enough. Should you happen to need more then go ahead and raise them (often these are referred to as subsidiary or auxiliary questions). The more questions you have though, the more work you will probably have to do and that can all get out of hand quite quickly.

Figure 2.1 **Getting started**

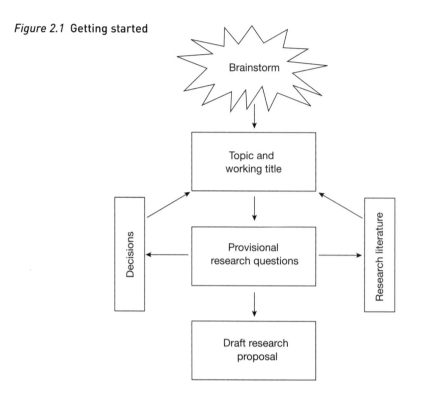

Practical task

Provisional research questions

Consider some of the following provisional research questions in detail. Which ones do you think might be easier to answer than others? Are they all researchable? Can you think of different ways of expressing the questions to better effect? Does changing the question materially alter the focus of the study (subtly or more dramatically)?

- Does using historical artefacts enhance teaching and learning?

- How do children use phonics to spell words?

- How do children's misconceptions in science affect later concept development?

- Is children's play gender specific?

- Is national assessment any more or less reliable than teacher assessment?

- Do friendship groups work any better than ability groups?

- Are summer born individuals academically disadvantaged?

- Is 'celebrity culture' impacting on children's aspirations and expectations?

- Does teacher language really make a difference in behaviour management?

- What is the educational value attached to museum visits?

- What do children have to say about school?

- Do learning disability centres address the educational needs of the disabled?

- Can role play help develop conflict resolution skills?

- Is inclusion a good idea?

- What do children use their computers for at home?

From the examples of research questions presented, it should be possible to see how you start to get drawn closer and closer to considering how you might approach the research and, in turn, thinking about particular methods of data collection and analysis.

Originality

When you start your individual research project and begin to explore the research literature available you might be tempted into thinking that you have to submit something original which makes a significant contribution to the field of educational research as a whole. Though in many instances this can and does happen it is not usually a requirement when studying education or training to be a teacher for the first time. It happens because the term 'originality' in educational research can be taken to mean the generation, development or production of something new, either from your own work or a reinterpretation of the work of others. So, while your work, or at least a part of it, could easily contain something new and original, it is important to remember that what counts most is for you to demonstrate that you are capable of carrying out an individual research project to completion, pretty much on your own and to an acceptable standard as determined by your own course criteria. This is the usual basis upon which your work will be marked or graded.

Organising and managing time

The amount of time you have available to you to undertake and complete your individual research project will depend entirely on your own course requirements and expectations. You may have been alerted to the individual research project months in advance of its anticipated start date and starting early will certainly help. Juggling the workload for this and everything else you will inevitably have to do alongside it can be difficult. Your individual research project will also have to be juggled around your own personal circumstances. You may have other family members or friends to consider, childcare arrangements to make, a job to hold down, or all of these things and more besides. The point is that you will need to organise and manage your time effectively and efficiently. This requires you to be able to look ahead and anticipate what you need to do and by when. The eventual mark or grade you receive for your individual research project will no doubt contribute significantly to your overall course performance and it's worth making sure to take care that this one thing gets all the attention it deserves. One way of ensuring that time is organised and managed well is to construct a time-flow chart showing where all of the most likely phases of your project fit into the term or semester. These phases include:

- focusing on a topic and working title;

- raising a provisional research question;

- searching for, retrieving and reviewing relevant literature;

- writing a research proposal outlining a basic research plan;

- identifying an approach and method for collecting data;

- trialling everything in a pilot study to find out what works and what doesn't;

- collecting and analysing data;

- drafting work, writing up and submitting.

Time-flow charts allow you to see the available time ahead of you and, when annotated fully, where targets, pressure points and deadlines lie. In addition to a time-flow chart, it might be useful to keep a diary or mark up a calendar too. Never leave anything to chance. But try not to squeeze everything in too tightly either. Something will always crop up resulting in delays. Oddly enough, it's often a good idea to start right at the end of the project with the submission date and work backwards. This has the advantage of making sure that you haven't bitten off any more than you can chew and that your plans are realistic.

In addition to time, of course, there will be other factors and resource implications attached to your work.

- Financial (e.g. photocopying, buying equipment, postage, binding).

- Access (e.g. travel, ethics, permission, police checks).

- Expertise (e.g. specific research methods, use of data handling software).

Each additional factor that you can think of will help determine the viability of your individual research project at an early stage leaving you with plenty of time to change direction should it become necessary.

Project phase	Teaching (weeks)												Assessment (weeks)		
	1	2	3	4	5	6	7	8	9	10	11	12	13	14	15
Topic/title	■	■	■												
Question		■	■	■											
Literature		■	■	■	■	■	■	■	■						
Proposal				■	■										
Approach/method					■	■									
Pilot							■								
Data collection							■	■							
Data analysis									■	■	■	■			
Draft writing			■	■	■	■	■	■	■	■	■	■			
Writing up/submit										■	■			■	

Table 2.1 Classroom-based individual research project time-flow chart for a typical semester

Practical task

Planning ahead

Consider your own individual research project in terms of the 'typical' phases of project management outlined here.

- Draw up your own time-flow chart taking care to ensure that it meets the requirements of your own individual circumstances.

- Add in all of your other course requirements and the deadlines you have to meet.

You now have a clear idea of the task that lies ahead. Have you remembered to build in some time to allow for those inevitable delays?

Developing a research proposal

Writing a research proposal, whether a formal requirement of your own course or not, is just good practice. Your own research proposal will take you well beyond initial brainstorming and help you to clarify your thoughts and ideas and to record these for discussion with others including your supervisor. Your supervisor will almost certainly wish to discuss your research with you in detail and having a research proposal helps. At this point, it may also be the first time that you begin to consider regulations surrounding the individual research project, details of which will probably be found in your course handbook. One of the most annoying things about research proposals, however, is that you are quite likely to be asked for one by your supervisor before you ever get to the lecture or seminar on the approach or method that works best for you. Your research proposal should, nevertheless, be completed with reference to at least the following sections.

- A working title.

- A provisional research question.

- An action plan.

- Sample literature.

- Ethical considerations.

A common mistake in presenting a working title is to write one out which is unfeasibly long, unnecessarily complicated and just badly constructed. Keep your working title simple and to the point. A provisional research question is critical in any research project as already indicated. The key to a good research question is to ensure that it is obviously researchable. Remember, your individual research project is likely to be small-scale and carried out over a relatively short period of time.

There is a limit to what you can achieve. An action plan should really set out to justify the choice of topic, approach and research method. You should also give some consideration to the location of the work if this is known, who will be involved if your work is classroom-based in particular, the amount and type of data you need to collect, and how you anticipate the project unfolding. If you find that you are including a wide range of different research methods for a whole manner of different things then your study might well be too ambitious. It's easy to try to collect too much of everything. Include your time-flow chart for reference. If you've already started to visit the library and locate relevant literature then include a summary of this too. All research requires some consideration of ethics even if library-based. Classroom-based research attached to a placement will certainly need a clear statement of ethical considerations especially if you intend to work with human participants either directly or indirectly. If considered particularly sensitive or intrusive your project may even require the approval of an ethics committee. Your supervisor will certainly work through ethics with you as well as ensuring that your work meets all course requirements. Try not to worry about the research proposal. The key term is 'proposal'. It will change like everything else so far.

Worked example

A first research proposal

The task

Rebecca was a final year student looking to progress on to a PGCE (Primary) course once her undergraduate work was over. Rebecca decided to focus her attention on the topic of mathematics education and on children's understanding of mathematical terms in particular. Her individual research project had to be completed over a fifteen week semester which included a short placement in a primary school. This example of a research proposal was prepared by Rebecca in time for her first of five research project tutorials and comes annotated with her supervisor's initial comments. Rebecca and her supervisor worked together to develop the research proposal over the weeks which followed and before she went into school to work with children and to collect data. A final version was eventually accepted and signed and dated by Rebecca and her supervisor who retained a copy for reference.

1. Working title

Understanding mathematical vocabulary at Key Stage 2. *[Fine.]*

2. Provisional research question

To what extent are Year 6 children aware of Key Stage 2 technical mathematical language as outlined by the National Numeracy Strategy vocabulary list? Is the technical vocabulary presented appropriate and suitable for children of this age? *[Are two questions really necessary? What do you mean by 'technical language', 'aware', 'appropriate' and 'suitable'? Examples?]*

3. Action plan

The mathematical vocabulary that primary children are expected to know and use is largely taken for granted. *[By whom?]* But what is this assumption actually based on? I plan to administer a questionnaire designed by me with a list of 15 technical mathematical words drawn from the National Numeracy Strategy vocabulary list to 30–60 Year 6 pupils in the middle 50% of the year group in my placement school between the end November and mid-December. *[Do any questionnaires already exist? Which words? On what basis are they being selected? Why 30–60 children? What do you mean by the middle 50%.]* I will ask the children if they recognise the words, find out if they can illustrate the words in mathematical terms and then find out if they can describe what the words mean verbally. *[This seems like more than a questionnaire to me.]*

4. Sample literature

My literature search so far has been limited but I have found a small number of useful sources dating back to 1976 and something even earlier by Vygotsky *[In what ways are these sources useful?]*:

Austin, J. L. and Howson, A. G. (1979) Language and Mathematical Education. *Educational Studies in Mathematics*, 10(2): 161–197.

Department for Education and Skills (2000) *The National Numeracy Strategy: Mathematical Vocabulary.* London: DfES Publications.

Earp, N. W. and Tanner, G. W. (1980) Mathematics and Language. *Arithmetic Teacher*, 28(4): 32–38.

Nicholson, A. R. (1977) Mathematics and Language. *Mathematics in School*, 6(5): 32–34.

Oldfield, C. (1996) The Language of Mathematics. *Mathematics in School*, 25(5): 22–23.

Otterburn, M. K. and Nicholson, A. R. (1976) The Language of CSE Mathematics. *Mathematics in School*, 5(5):18–20.

Preston, M. (1978) The Language of Early Mathematical Experience. *Mathematics in School*, 7(4): 31–32.

Raiker, A. (2002) Spoken Language and Mathematics. *Cambridge Journal of Education*, 32(1): 45–60.

Vygotsky, L. S. (1962) *Thought and Language*. Massachusetts: The Massachusetts Institute of Technology Press.

5. Ethical considerations

The project requires access to between 30 and 60 Year 6 children via placement school (details of the class not yet fully known). Already checked over the phone with head teacher and class teacher and okay. Confidentiality and anonymity will be guaranteed by changing the name of the school and all individuals concerned. *[Consider sampling technique and don't forget to ask and inform the children!]*

Supervision

At the start of your individual research project you will almost certainly be assigned a supervisor. You may even get a choice. Levels of supervision vary from place to place and course to course. At the very least, your entitlement to supervision might run to a few one-to-one or group tutorials. Full details will probably be found in your course handbook. There is every likelihood that your supervisor may not be an expert in your particular topic but he or she will be sufficiently experienced in educational research to apply what they know and guide you satisfactorily. Supervisors are there to help and your success reflects well on them too. But the whole point of an individual research project is that it is your own work and carried out by you working on your own as far as possible. Your supervisor will certainly lead you in the 'right' direction but he or she will certainly not do your project for you or make decisions on your behalf. If you choose to ignore your supervisor's advice, which you are perfectly at liberty to do, you can't come back and moan if everything goes horribly wrong (though an experienced supervisor may still try to retrieve the situation with you). Whether your tutorials are formal or informal:

- establish what you both want out of your time together and don't be shy about asking for help and advice;

- don't ever be late or miss a tutorial without good reason or without letting your supervisor know (you should expect the same courtesy in return);

- turn up fully prepared at all times;

- find out when draft work needs to be in and when feedback can be expected (if this provision is made available to you).

Occasionally you may have to change supervisor part way through your project. There may be many reasons for this. Sometimes, it may be felt that someone else is better placed to help supervise you or your supervisor may just become unavailable. It is extremely unlikely that you and your supervisor will 'fall out', but disputes and differences of opinion do occasionally happen. In such an unlikely event, follow any guidelines which deal with channels of communication in your course handbook. While the vast majority of relationships between students and supervisors work well your supervisor is, nevertheless, not available to you at all times. Do not make e-mail demands of your supervisor if he or she as asked you not to communicate with them in this way and don't phone your supervisor at midnight when you're stuck even if he or she did give you their home phone number for emergencies. Strange though it may seem, looking out for you isn't everything that they have to do.

Research ups and downs

It is essential that you identify the right environment to work in quickly. This may be at home, in the library or even where you buy your coffee (maybe with the added bonus of free internet access). It may be noisy and busy, which is just what you like, or quiet and calm. Above all it should allow you be comfortable and productive, however this applies to you. Whoever said research is 99% perspiration and 1% inspiration got it just about right. While your own individual research project will inevitably be carried out on something which interests you, it's highly unlikely you'll be interested in it all of the time. Your own motivation, along with many of the other personal attributes we all share, will naturally wax and wane. What is important is that you recognise this and, where possible, try to keep everything in perspective. Everything really will return to normal eventually. If you should happen to experience a personal problem which begins to impact adversely on your work, however, it is essential that you mention this to your supervisor or to a member of staff with responsibility for student support without delay. Your supervisor in particular, while able to read the subtleties in student mood and body language with uncanny precision, is not a mind reader. Personal illness or illness in a family member, bereavement, unforeseen legal matters and other unfortunate circumstances may give legitimate grounds for an extension should this become necessary. Formal evidence will probably be required. Guidelines for dealing with such matters will almost certainly appear in your course handbook.

Research ethics

Research helps to move things forward and to make things better. But you can't just do research at any cost. As such, your individual research project should be carried out in an ethically proper manner from start to finish. This means ensuring that all appropriate steps are taken to protect the interests, status, values and beliefs of all participants and organisations, including you, from harm (e.g. physical, social, psychological, professional). These days, ethical considerations also extend to observing copyright restrictions and taking care to avoid all forms of cheating including plagiarism. It's all too easy in the rush to get your individual research project underway to forget that whatever you do will always have an impact of one sort or another and that there may be risks attached which could easily be avoided. All individual research projects, but particularly those which are classroom-based and require you to work with children, require careful ethical consideration. Your individual research project may seem straightforward and neither sensitive nor intrusive to you but others might not see it that way. Your supervisor will certainly lead you towards any relevant guidelines which govern research ethics on your own particular course and there may even be an ethics statement in your own course handbook. Even at the proposal stage of your work, you should give very careful thought to at least the following.

- The purpose of your work and why it needs to be undertaken at all.

- Obtaining informed consent from all relevant parties.

- Ensuring rigour, accuracy and impartiality in data collection, analysis and reporting.

- Respecting privacy, anonymity and confidentiality.

- Avoiding betrayal and deception.

- Establishing ownership, 'voice' and the intended readership.

- Maintaining awareness of cultural sensitivities.

- Assessing personal and professional impact.

Data protection legislation also helps enforce an ethical approach to all forms of educational research by ensuring that all personal data and other information relating to identifiable individuals is collected and treated with care and integrity.

- You should only seek to collect data which you actually need to collect.

- You should keep all data safe, secure and protected from loss or theft at all times.

- You should never distribute, disclose or use any data beyond the stated intentions of your research.

- You should never attempt to falsify, alter or misrepresent findings.

- You should destroy or delete all personal data once you are sure it is no longer required.

When working in a school, for example, common-sense dictates that you should also discuss your project with the head teacher who is in a position to offer more 'local' advice. Do this as far in advance of the pilot and data collection phases of your work as possible. The head teacher may still require you to write to the parents or guardians of children for informed consent if, indeed, children are involved in any way. If this is the case, your letter should at least outline:

- who you are and where you study;

- what your work entails and why it needs to be carried out;

- what it is you are looking to collect and how you intend to go about collecting it;

- how you will ensure that the children's 'rights' will be respected and privacy, anonymity and confidentiality maintained.

Letters granting permission should be returned signed and dated and kept in a safe place. It is essential that you present your work to the children involved too and to be aware that any intended participant has the 'right' to withdraw at any time or to refuse to have their image or voice recorded by whatever means regardless of adult consent having been obtained.

Reflective task

Ethical dilemmas

There are a great many professional associations which provide advice on research ethics including the British Educational Research Association (BERA). Access the ethics pages of BERA by visiting its website and read what it has to say carefully (follow BERA Publications to Guidelines):

- British Educational Research Association (2008) *BERA*. Available at: www.bera.ac.uk.

How does the information presented here compare alongside the ethics guidelines available in your own course handbook or the professional association related to the area of education you are specialising in or interested in? Which matches your own circumstances better?

Consider each of the following individual research project scenarios carefully. Using all of the ethics information now at your disposal, identify what ethical considerations, if any, need to be carefully attended to in each case (e.g. purpose, consent, impartiality, anonymity, confidentiality, betrayal, deception, ownership, 'voice', cultural sensitivities, impact). Discuss with others how you might ensure that each situation was ethically sound:

- using a collection of images and artefacts to explore primary children's perceptions of different religious beliefs;

- relying on help from a fellow student to analyse and interpret your data because they know more about statistics than you do;

- identifying a primary school by name from its Ofsted report in the reference list of a project;

- assessing the reaction to failure by telling some children in school that they'd failed a test when in fact they'd passed it;

- gaining permission from a head teacher of a school or director of an outdoor centre, museum or gallery to carry out research alongside a class teacher or education officer who has made it clear to you they are not interested in being involved;

- researching the changing face of ICT in contemporary culture by exploring social networking (chat rooms, *YouTube*, *MySpace* and *Facebook*) and the problems attached to bullying, grooming and gaming;

- interviewing children at school who did not bring back their consent form from parents;

- uncovering a serious breakdown in communication between the senior management team of a school and its class teachers knowing that the Chair of Governors has asked to read your report;

- discovering that another student on your course has falsified data in their report to make their findings look better;

- interviewing infant children who didn't seem to be fully aware of what you were doing.

Within the context of research ethics in education, what do you think is meant by protecting human participants, including you, from physical, social, psychological or professional harm?

Summary of key points

Get a clear focus on what you want to do as soon as possible but look out for anything which might make your project an unlikely starter.

Come up with a working title and at least one provisional research question as soon as you can.

Begin to access the research literature and any information available via your own professional association as soon as possible. This will help with focus and with planning.

Time can be your enemy as well as your friend. Don't leave everything to the last minute. Construct a time-flow chart for yourself and build in a time contingency for unforeseen delays.

Consider writing a research proposal even if you are not formally required to do so. Don't try to be clever. Keep everything simple, straightforward and doable.

Discuss all of your thoughts and ideas with others but particularly your supervisor. You will need all the help you can get in the early stages of your project.

Try to keep the ups and downs of your work in perspective but don't let the downs get out of control.

Working in an ethical manner is paramount. Take great care to plan your work with ethical considerations very much to the fore. Adhere to course ethics requirements and 'local' circumstances at all times.

Further reading

Some useful background to planning research can be found in Davies (2007) and Walliman (2004). Both are highly readable but not particularly contextualised within education. There are three particularly valuable books which deal with research ethics. These are by Oliver (2003), Fraser et al. (2003) and Farrell (2005). Fraser et al. (2003) and Farrell (2005) in particular discuss working ethically with very young children.

Davies, M.B. (2007) *Doing a successful research project using qualitative or quantitative methods*. Basingstoke: Palgrave Macmillan.

Farrell, A. (ed) (2005) *Ethical research with children*. Maidenhead: Open University Press.

Fraser, S., Lewis, V., Ding, S., Kellett, M. and Robinson, C. (eds) (2003) *Doing research with children and young people*. London: Sage.

Oliver, P. (2003) *The student's guide to research ethics*. Maidenhead: Open University Press.

Walliman, N. (2004) *Your undergraduate dissertation: the essential guide to success*. London: Sage.

3. Looking at literature

Learning outcomes

Accessing the research literature not only helps to find a focus for your work, it attends to an essential and important aspect of the individual research project, the literature review. You might be misled into thinking that the literature review is something that shouldn't take too long and that getting it out of the way will be easy, but nothing could be further from the truth. By having read this chapter and completed the tasks within it, you will:

- know what a literature review is and the purpose it serves;

- be able to adopt appropriate strategies to search for, retrieve and summarise relevant literature and how to incorporate it into your work;

- improve your ability to read and write reflectively, critically and analytically;

- be aware of the strengths and limitations of web-based information obtained via the internet.

The literature review

Looking at literature extends well beyond the need to find a focus for your work. It helps to complete what is known as the literature review. It is extremely unlikely that you will choose to settle on a topic that has never been written about before and so it is important for you to engage with *the field*. The literature review can cause a few problems for up until now you may have read only the materials given out to you on your own course or which you've located yourself when prompted with a ready-made reading list. Now you have to go and find things to read for yourself. The literature review forms a fairly conventional part of all individual research projects and serves a number of different functions.

- It introduces the reader to your topic and contextualises your contribution in terms of where and how it *fits in* and how you intend to go about doing it (sometimes incorporating a theoretical or analytical framework).

- It demonstrates that you as the researcher are familiar with *the field* surrounding your topic and what has already been said and done, particularly with respect to the approaches adopted by others and their interpretation of findings.

- It affords you the opportunity to demonstrate scholarship in your ability to reflect upon, evaluate and write critically and analytically (that is to be rigorously discriminating and to seek out errors, inconsistencies or flaws in logic, reasoning and argument) by identifying where the literature is thin, where potential gaps in current knowledge exist, what issues, arguments, debates and opinions have arisen, and what questions or problems remain that you might wish to pursue and investigate.

There is some debate about whether or not a formal literature review is always required. Sometimes, for example, a literature review of sorts can appear as part of a project's introduction or be subsumed within the main findings. But while studying education or training to be a teacher for the first time, it would be wise to follow convention unless otherwise directed by your own course handbook. The expression *literature review* can also be misleading when carrying out research in certain specialist areas. If your work focuses on music or art education, for example, your main sources of information may not be literature-based at all but involve sounds and images. While there may be some case for adjusting the title of this part of your project, the underlying purpose and principles of *review* remain the same. Don't do anything that might be considered unorthodox without consulting your supervisor first.

Practical task

Literature reviews in educational research

The literature review is an essential part of any individual research project but it can cause problems. Common questions include:

- What is it for?

- How long should it be?

- How many sources do I need to use?

- Do I need to use journals?

- What if I can't find anything?

There are no easy answers to these questions, of course, for each literature review is specific to the topic chosen for investigation and the specific requirements of each individual course. There are no shortcuts either. Take another visit to where the current education journals are on display in your library. The easiest way to get familiar with the literature review is to simply look at as many as you can and read them for yourself. Different journals and different authors adopt very different styles but the purpose and principles are generally the same in every case. Consider each literature review you find in terms of the function it serves.

Carrying out a literature review is a very specific task within an individual research project and this can take up a considerable amount of time. Literature has to be found, retrieved, read, summarised and reported. This should be factored into your planning so don't leave it until the last minute to do. The literature review isn't something that you can set out to do as a one-off either. The literature review will probably extend throughout the duration of your project, starting slowly, gaining pace early on and then tailing off as you approach writing-up. The more you get immersed, however, the more you'll want to find out. This contributes to the excitement of research. You just never know what you're going to find or where you'll find it. There is always the fear of missing something out, of course, and looking for literature can become obsessive, but you do have to decide when to stop searching and reading eventually. In addition to finding and using literature, you will also have to find ways or organising and managing it too.

From the very outset, and as you dig deeper and deeper, the whole search for literature may feel bewildering. You may find that what you have chosen to focus on has more literature than you can possibly cope with in the time available. You may find that there is hardly anything at all. This can be a good thing or a bad thing depending on your perspective. You certainly won't be expected to have read everything associated with your topic by any means, but if you overlook something particularly important it will probably be noticed. Do not underestimate the importance of the literature review. It's probably the one piece of draft writing your supervisor will ask to read and comment on, if such a service is made available to you, and the first section of the individual research project your supervisor will read in detail when finally submitted. The quality of the literature review often sets the tone for the rest of the project. While getting to grips with the literature review, you will certainly become more information literate than you are now.

Searching for and retrieving information

As has been mentioned before, your library really is your best friend and you need to get to know it and how to make the most out of it well. There you will find a *user guide* which concerns itself with searching for and retrieving information from the library catalogue together with a complete list of other resources and databases your library subscribes to in print and electronically. All of this information, together with other help and advice, will also be available to you via your library's website. If you are uncertain about how best to proceed in terms of accessing the resources at your disposal then make an appointment to speak with a librarian as a matter of priority.

By having already settled on a topic with a working title and a preliminary research question, you will already have some idea of what information you might be interested in looking for and where you might find it no matter how vague that idea might be. The search and retrieval process will certainly be easier as a result. The most common sources of information for literature reviews in individual research projects include:

- academic journals, textbooks and online databases;

- educational websites obtained via the internet;

- professional journals, newspapers and magazines (including the education sections of broadsheets, *The Times Educational Supplement* and *The Times Higher Education* – formerly the *Times Higher Education Supplement*);

- communication with authority figures in the field (including your supervisor, other academic staff teaching on your own course and academic staff in other institutions and organisations).

There are a great many others, of course, but these will do to begin with. It is essential in any form of research, however, to use the most credible academic sources available. Most of the relevant literature you need will therefore be found in academic journals, textbooks and online databases. If you are in the final year of an undergraduate course or following a one-year postgraduate course then the use of journals as a primary source of information will be expected and you shouldn't need to be reminded. Many journals and textbooks can be located and accessed electronically depending on what your library subscribes to. Search for everything you can find that's topic-specific initially and widen your search from there. While there is no simple answer to how many sources or which type of source you need, you should try to access as broad and balanced a range of literature as possible. If all of your sources turn out to be generic websites then this probably says something about you and the limitations of your search and retrieval technique.

Practical task

Search and retrieval

With your topic, working title and provisional research question in mind, it's time to begin the formal literature review. These days, most research literature and other sources of information are available in printed and electronic forms. It's a matter of personal preference which you choose to consult but:

- start with your library catalogue before turning to an internet search engine – your search is more likely to find credible and authoritative educational materials that you have immediate access to;

- if you are aware of any relevant authors or actual titles of pieces of writing then search for these first – otherwise use different combinations of key words and phrases to avoid missing anything obvious;

- if you find too little, widen your search by adjusting the words and phrases accordingly;

- if you find too much, close your search down by being more specific;

- consult the help and advice pages of your library catalogue to refine your work.

While it is tempting to rush to e-journals and e-books, manually browsing journals and textbooks in the library, particularly once you've identified the journals most likely to contain the information you might be interested in or the shelves where certain authors or types of textbook appear, can keep you up to date and draw you into other literature which electronic searches cannot always do. You also get to meet and interact with other library-users too! The very act of reviewing literature will result in the accumulation of vast amounts of information

Practical task continued

but it is essential that this is organised, summarised and presented coherently. Once you have exhausted what your own library catalogue has to offer, turn your attention to online databases such as the British Education Index (BEI) or the Education Resources and Information Center (ERIC). Use their help and advice facilities to refine your search as necessary.

Academic journals (in print or electronic forms) are peer-reviewed publications which present collections of articles in all sorts of areas of interest in order to advance knowledge and expertise. They are published at regular intervals throughout the year. It is important to keep looking at the education journals regularly to keep up to date. It's easy to get stuck looking at a small range of specialist journals for relevant articles but articles on all sorts get published elsewhere too. A useful short-list of useful education journals to keep on top of might include:

- *British Educational Research Journal*;

- *Research Papers in Education*;

- *British Journal of Educational Studies*;

- *Educational Studies*;

- *Research in Education*;

- *Teaching and Teacher Education*;

- *Early Years*;

- *The Curriculum Journal*;

- *Oxford Review of Education*;

- *Cambridge Journal of Education*;

- *Education 3–13*.

Education 3–13 is a particularly useful journal to start with as the articles it publishes are generally quite short and the journal is aimed at reaching a wide audience. It's also useful to consult the research pages of professional associations including the ones attached to any subject area you are specialising in or interested in. Sometimes review articles or special issue editions of journals are made available and these can be particularly valuable if your topic happens to be included. Once you begin to locate some relevant journal articles, pay close attention to the reference lists which appear at the end. As you become more skilled at working with journals you may begin to notice that the same authors and articles get more attention than others. These are clearly sources that you need to track down and read as a matter of priority. Journals are not normally available on loan and you will need to photocopy any articles you want or download them if available online (subject to copyright restrictions). If anything is immediately unavailable to you, your library will be able to get it via inter-library loan (sometimes for a small fee). Professional articles are of relevance and use too, of course, but these may not contain the information you need at the right level of detail.

Academic textbooks (in print or electronic form) are fantastic sources of information but can date quite quickly. They become dated because they often, though not always, tend to draw on what appears in journals for their subject matter and because the educational world has a tendency to change faster than textbooks can be written and published. This is one reason why keeping an eye on journals is so important. Always check that you are looking at the most recent edition of a textbook. Sometimes you have to do this by referring to the publisher's catalogue rather than your library catalogue. Always check the reference lists for other relevant sources. Textbooks can be borrowed from libraries, of course, but what you want may already be out on loan resulting in delay. As with articles in journals, your library will be able to get anything you need via inter-library loan.

Online databases are found via the internet. Some are freely available while others are subscription sites and password protected. Your library will know which is which and can advise you on how to obtain access. The British Education Index or BEI (www.leeds.ac.uk/bei) is a particularly valuable resource which provides details of the titles and abstracts of articles, conference papers and other research reports covering education and training in over 300 relevant journals and other publications produced in the UK. While browsing the BEI through your own library catalogue electronically, you may be able to access full-text versions of relevant materials directly. Otherwise you will have to look for it elsewhere. The Education Resources and Information Center or ERIC (www.eric.ed.gov) is the US equivalent of the BEI. ERIC contains a broader range of educational resources than the BEI, indexing over 600 relevant journals and other publications from around the world. It also has the advantage of providing links to full-text versions of relevant materials in many instances. Your library will provide details of other online databases it subscribes to and how to access and use them on request.

Using the internet

Websites available via the internet are both a blessing and a curse in all search and retrieval senses attached to project work. They are a blessing in that you can locate a great deal of valuable information in addition to that found in journals, textbooks and online databases. They are a curse in that the internet is unregulated and many of the websites it will take you to contain information that is inaccurate or simply not true. Anyone can own a website and put on it what they like, even you. Many websites claim to be educational in nature and look both professional and authoritative but simply lack academic credibility. Sadly, this is also true of many commercial sites which are, after all, commercial for a purpose. Using the internet requires great skill and care in determining what you choose to rely on and use. The thoughtless and indiscriminate use of the internet can lead to poor scholarship and shallow learning resulting in the award of low project marks or even fail grades. It's easy to fall into the trap, for example, of confusing finding information with understanding what it has to tell you and interrogating it thoroughly. Evaluating the credibility of websites is not at all easy but the following generally accepted questions may help.

- Is the author clearly identified and appropriately qualified to comment?

- Is the author attached to a reputable academic or commercial organisation you recognise or are familiar with?

- Is the nature and purpose of the website clear?

- Is the material presented research-based and if so how was it obtained?

- Is the material presented discussed in a balanced way and referenced using academic sources in a conventional manner?

- Is there any evidence that the website or the material presented has been peer-reviewed or rigorously and independently vetted by some other means?

- When was the material posted and is it current?

Using the internet will certainly test your search skills and powers of discrimination to the full. But remember:

- relying on the internet as your sole means of searching for information is just an accident waiting to happen, the consequences of which have far reaching academic implications;

- because the information you are looking for doesn't appear as a result of your search doesn't mean that it doesn't exist and that it isn't worth investing the time to look for it elsewhere.

Plagiarism as a result of internet misuse is sadly but very definitely on the increase as more and more students intentionally or unintentionally cut and paste from websites directly into their own work without proper acknowledgement. Just as this is easy to do, it is just as easy to find and without the need for specialised detection software. You have been warned.

(Reflective task)

Becoming an 'Internet Detective'

Internet search engines look virtually everywhere they can for virtually everything you ask them to look for. In order to get the most out of a search engine you need to be familiar with all of the tools it offers to help you refine your search. Take a close look at the following:

- *Google* (www.google.co.uk);

- *YaHoo!* (www.yahoo.com);

- *altavista* (www.altavista.com);

- *Ask* (http://uk.ask.com);

- your own preferred search engine if different from any of these.

How do they compare in terms of search tips and advanced search facilities? Google, for example, offers *Google Scholar*, *Google Advanced Search* and *Google Book Search* which are all particularly helpful and you may wish to try using these in preference to *Google* itself.

Put each search engine to the test if only to convince yourself of the problem each one can generate for you. Exploring children's learning styles as VAK (visual, auditory, kinaesthetic) is a common project topic for many students. Use each search engine in turn to look for information using different combinations of the words and phrases *VAK*, *learning styles*, *education* and *schools* and log the number of hits returned. You may be surprised to find that it can range from quite literally thousands to millions which is not much use in an individual research project with a limited time frame. Now take some time to evaluate some of the websites that appear at the top of the list using the website evaluation questions presented here. Hopefully by now you can appreciate the scale of the task ahead of you when using the internet. Among the articles and reports looking critically at learning styles in education are those by Coffield et al. (2004), Cassidy (2004), Demos (2005) and Sharp et al. (2008). Do any of these sources appear anywhere on the hits you obtained? Now that you know about them, use *Google* or any of the search engines above to try to track down full details and full-text versions. How easy is this to do? Familiarity with the literature surrounding your topic isn't necessarily something that will come easily. But the more familiar with it you get, the easier all of your searches will become and the less likely it will be that you will use something completely inappropriate.

In order to become more experienced at using the internet as a source of academic information, access the Internet Detective at the following location:

- University of Bristol (2008) *Internet Detective*. Available at: www.vts.intute.ac.uk/detective.

Following the online tutorials this website provides, are you web-wise? Consider your own use of the web in relation to what is presented about the *good*, the *bad* and the *ugly*. Are you sure what it means now to be an Internet Detective?

Effective reading, note-taking and writing

As indicated earlier, the literature review is a formal piece of academic writing which demonstrates that you have not only read around your topic in some detail but that you are capable of selecting, organising, clarifying and presenting the work of others in a reflective, critical and analytical way. It is not always clear from the outset what form the literature review will take or how it might be structured and presented (e.g. chronologically or by some other means) as it's almost impossible to know in advance what literature will be available to you. You will also have a limited amount of time and words to play with and you will need to make some tough decisions about what to include and at what level of detail. All in all, writing the literature review, like the whole project itself, can prove to be a painful process. Just remember, though, that writing for most of us is painful most of the time in one way or another so you're in good company. The pain isn't helped by the fact that you will certainly find yourself wading through sometimes highly theoretical, ideological, technical and far from transparent texts, possibly for the first time. But there are a few things you can do to minimise the pain.

- Start early, set clear goals and use as wide a range of credible academic sources as you can find.

- Pay particular attention to how other authors have approached writing literature reviews.

- Save words by using tables, charts, graphs and other forms of illustration to summarise information where appropriate.

- Try to present a logical, coherent and easy to follow *story* from start to finish.

- Don't forget to let the reader know, usually towards the end, where your own work is located or *sits* within it all.

- Draft your literature review over and over until it *feels* right and be prepared to act on any feedback from your supervisor should feedback be made available to you.

Underpinning the quality of your literature review is your ability to read and take notes efficiently and effectively and to turn those notes into narrative. Never rely on memory. It will only let you down. There are several strategies available to you to improve your reading technique. You probably use them all the time but never give them a second's thought.

- Establish quickly how much time and attention you can devote to each information source.

- Read abstracts and conclusions of journal articles or summary chapters of textbooks and reports if available to determine general content and meaning and whether or not the text is immediately relevant and likely to be of further use.

- Skim or speed read the whole text or sections of it very quickly looking for key words or content to identify areas or chunks of particular interest which might be worth returning to (e.g. the introduction, the literature review, the methodology or the presentation and interpretation of findings).

- Scan the areas or chunks of text of particular interest and read these to work out exactly what is being said in more detail.

- If the source seems particularly valuable, read the entire text sentence by sentence carefully from start to finish.

Becoming familiar with your sources is important and it is not impossible that you might find yourself returning to read some of them over and over. This is perfectly normal.

Good note-taking will help break up your reading into manageable proportions, help you to focus on, clarify and understand what counts most and help you to gather the information you need in a succinct manner. There are several note-taking strategies available to you. As with reading, you probably use them all the time but never give them a second's thought.

- Underlining or highlighting key words or phrases of interest, possibly with a view to selecting suitable quotations (though quotations should be used sparingly).

- Annotating copies of text or the margins around it directly with comments, questions, thoughts and where similar points are made elsewhere (never write directly on to the articles in journals or textbooks in your library – this is an act of vandalism and an offence which carries a strict penalty).

- Preparing lengthier and systematic reviews of text.

Taking notes effectively and accurately will also help you to transform what you read into your own words and avoid plagiarism. If you do feel the need to copy out a lot of text word for word then remember to place all of it in quotation marks and acknowledge the source and page numbers to remind you. Preparing lengthier reviews of text systematically usually involves:

- writing down full reference details of the source (author, date, title, details of publication);

- providing a general overview;

- considering the strengths, weaknesses and limitations in the literature review, the methods employed to collect and handle data and the presentation and interpretation of findings;

- looking out for inconsistencies, unsubstantiated claims, personal opinions, emerging issues, arguments and debates;

- considering any links with other work.

Adopting a systematic approach such as the one presented here will take you beyond presenting a simple description of sources which you should try to avoid at all costs.

Armed with all of your notes, the trick then is to move from notes to narrative, blending everything you've read into a coherent and well worked *story* and linking ideas from different sources together or cross-referencing clearly without unnecessary repetition. Many marks or grades are won and lost on how well you do this yet there is no formula for how to achieve it other than learning by reading as much as you can and practising. Sometimes the pressure of having to write within a tight timeframe causes writer's block. This is a very real phenomenon which happens to the best of writers from time to time. Writer's block can be very distressing in severe cases and you should always let your supervisor know if it happens to you. Most of the time, the problem involves committing pen to paper (or finger to keyboard). If it helps:

- try not to worry about the coherency and flow of your writing initially;

- blitz everything that you think you are trying to say on to paper or on to screen or flit from one to the other;

- avoid dwelling for too long on the construction and meaning behind each and every sentence or paragraph you write;

- tidy up any apparent ramblings later;

- try to see the *big picture*;

- if all else fails and you have time on your side, walk away for an hour or a day or two, the break sometimes helps the brain sort it out.

Worked example

From notes to narrative

The task

Julia's notes

When taking notes, you should try to write down everything you need first time. A good way of remembering how to do this systematically is to run through a simple set of prompts. You can make up your own, of course, but with care and practise 'Who?', 'Why?', 'Where?', 'How?' and 'What?' just about covers it all. Julia, a primary PGCE student, was getting quite good at this. Interested in finding out about what children think about their teachers, Julia happened across an article by Hutchings et al. (2008). Her notes from the article are presented for illustration.

1. Who?

Hutchings, M., Carrington, B., Francis, B., Skelton, C., Read, B. and Hall, I. (2008) Nice and kind, smart and funny: what children like and want to emulate in their teachers. *Oxford Review of Education*, 34(2): 135–157.

2. Why?

The study was intended to explore what children like and want to emulate in their teachers as suggested by the title but actually addressed in detail the popular and often widely accepted assumption that more male teachers should be recruited to primary schools to serve as role models for boys.

3. Where?

The study involved over 300 Year 3 children in 51 different classes in 34 different schools located in the south-east and north-east of England.

4. How?

Of the 51 different classes, 25 were taught by male teachers and 26 by female teachers. Data collection took place by classroom observation followed up with individual interviews. The questions: What do you like about your class teacher?

Are there ways in which you would like to be like your class teacher? Can you think of anybody you know you would like to be like when you grow up? All interviews were audio-recorded and transcribed in full and analysed qualitatively using Nvivo. Parental consent was obtained in advance. 7 and 8-year-olds were chosen as gender identities were considered well established by this age.

5. What?

The overall findings were complex. At one level, some children based their likes on masculine and feminine traits and characteristics as appropriate depending on context (e.g. nice, friendly, formed good relationships, smart appearance, intelligent). 'Sex-role socialisation' was not all it seemed to be. Children appeared to want a good teacher regardless of whether they were male or female though some 'gendered patterns' emerged. Overall conclusion, no need for male role models but for all teachers to be 'gender aware', to avoid behaving in gender-stereotyped ways and to respond to boys and girls equally in class.

This is a good set of notes and in time Julia would be able to comment further on the significance of this article alongside others in her work.

The task

Jonathan's narrative

Notes are all very well, of course, but you have to turn notes into narrative eventually. In an individual research project requiring a review of primary teachers' curricular expertise in science, Jonathan, in the final year of his BA course with QTS, first located a fairly recent article by Parker (2004). The reference list provided Jonathan with an opportunity to exemplify some of the issues raised by tracking down an earlier article co-written by the same author (Parker and Heywood 1998). This, in turn, led to further exemplification with reference to other related works. Quite fortuitously, and by simply browsing the titles appearing in relevant journals in the library, Jonathan happened across the emergence of a particularly forceful argument between Summers and Mant (1995b) and Golby et al. (1995). It is important to note here that a simple Internet search may not have taken Jonathan as deeply into the literature and that some important sources may have been overlooked as a result. Jonathan proceeded to prepare a first draft. His references are included for completeness.

1. The story

In the first of two Primary School Teachers and Science (PSTS) project studies, Mant and Summers (1993) described the outcomes of interviews designed to explore primary teachers' knowledge and understanding of the Earth's place in the Universe as it existed in the National Curriculum at that time. Working with an opportunity sample of 20 volunteers from schools mostly in and around Oxfordshire (15 women and 5 men varying widely in age, science background and teaching experience), individuals were probed about their observations of the sky and their explanations for day and night, the seasons, the phases of the Moon and the Solar System and wider Universe. Mant and Summers reported that:

- the teachers involved did not have good observational knowledge of what happens in the sky and at times appeared to work backwards from what they thought they should see rather than drawing on first hand observational experience;

- most of the teachers were unable to explain, or gave erroneous explanations for, phenomena associated with the Earth-Sun-Moon System;

- most of the mental models of the Solar System and wider Universe were not in accord with any scientific model;

- aware of their situation, most of the teachers expressed dissatisfaction with existing levels of confidence and knowledge and understanding and indicated the need for support.

In more detail, while 15 teachers (75%) gave scientific accounts for day and night, only 4 (20%) gave scientific accounts of the reasons for seasonal change and only 2 (10%) gave scientific accounts of the phases of the Moon. 4 teachers (20%) were found to hold a consistent mental model of the Solar System and wider Universe as a whole and the Earth's place within it. Broadly similar findings were reported from a second study which was conducted using a survey questionnaire with another opportunity sample of 66 practising teachers also from schools in and around Oxfordshire and 54 graduate trainees who had just completed their primary PGCE at Westminster College, Oxford (Summers and Mant 1995a). Despite the short passage of time between studies, there still existed a mismatch between participants' existing knowledge and understanding and the requirements of the National Science Curriculum in this area.

Not entirely at ease with their approach, Golby et al. (1995) strongly criticised the work of Mant and Summers (1993) which they described as 'typical of its kind' and suggested that Mant and Summers set out to reveal that primary teachers have gaps in their knowledge which were detrimental to their practice. Golby et al. made a strong link between this 'deficit model' and the requirements outlined for improvement and a transmission-reception view of teaching and learning which ran contrary to that based upon constructivism and was therefore unsound. Golby et al. implied that Mant and Summers may have misled participants as to the nature of their enquiry and that this was ethically improper. Golby et al. also pointed out that Mant and Summers failed to explore or to acknowledge what teachers 'can do' neglecting, for example, how teachers might actually have prepared for what they had to teach. In an equally strong response, Summers and Mant (1995b) vigorously rejected all of the claims made against them, arguing forcefully that good subject knowledge was an important prerequisite for good teaching, whatever the subject, that possessing good subject knowledge in no way implied a transmission-reception view of teaching and learning, and that Golby et al. misunderstood the role of subject knowledge in constructivist teaching. Summers and Mant also suggested that Golby et al. were somewhat 'confused' and misguided about the nature of science and science education. Summers and Mant accused Golby et al. of 'careless reading', 'inaccuracies' in reporting, being 'out-of-touch' and 'unwilling' to consider any evidence which might challenge their own preconceptions of what science is and what constitutes effective teaching and learning.

Careful reading of each work suggests that while, on balance, Summers and Mant might appear to hold the moral high ground on most issues raised, Golby et al. were perhaps also correct in drawing attention to what teachers 'can do', to the complexities of teaching and learning at all levels, and that a variety of alternative approaches may be valuable. Clearly there remains a need for empirical and evidence-based studies of acquiring curricular expertise within the complex, interactive nature of knowledge types in classroom situations. One potential solution was later provided by Parker and Heywood (1998) who wrote that:

> A fundamental principle of teacher education should be concerned with identifying and making explicit the underlying conceptual frameworks which the learner [the child in this case] is likely to have difficulty with in becoming encultured into the scientific interpretation of events. It is our contention that this objective is most effectively achieved in the teacher auditing his/her own learning when engaging with the concepts themselves. . . . Without insight into the learning process involved, subtle nuances that impact markedly on the capacity for learners to make the necessary links are lost. (518–519)

Despite decades of research, the 'problem' of teachers' curricular expertise in primary science appears to remain very much unresolved (see Parker 2004 for further details).

2. The references

Golby, M., Martin, A. and Porter, M. (1995) Some researchers' understanding of primary teaching: comments on Mant and Summers' 'Some primary school teachers' understanding of the Earth's place in the universe'. *Research Papers in Education*, 10(3): 297–302.

Mant, J. and Summers, M. (1993) Some primary school teachers' understanding of the Earth's place in the universe. *Research Papers in Education*, 8(1): 101–129.

Parker, J. (2004) The synthesis of subject and pedagogy for effective learning and teaching in primary science education. *British Educational Research Journal*, 30(6): 819–839.

Parker, J. and Heywood, D. (1998) The Earth and beyond: developing primary teachers' understanding of basic astronomical concepts. *International Journal of Science Education*, 20(5): 503–520.

Summers, M. and Mant, J. (1995a) A survey of British primary school teachers' understanding of the Earth's place in the universe. *Educational Research*, 37(1): 3–19.

Summers, M. and Mant, J. (1995b) A misconceived view of subject-matter knowledge in primary science: a response to Golby et al. 'Some researchers' understanding of primary teaching'. *Research Papers in Education*, 10(3): 303–307.

Jonathan has done a pretty good job of presenting a great deal of information from six articles to the reader in surprisingly few words (using 'Who?', 'Why?', 'Where?', 'How?' and 'What?'). The essence of the argument is clear and supported with evidence. Take a close look at the how Jonathan has incorporated and cited the work of the key authors into the text too, how words and phrases are quoted without the need for page numbers, and how the main quotation, with page numbers, is set apart from the main text (including the insertion of words in square brackets to help clarify meaning and how where text has been omitted is represented). The reference list is already in alphabetical order and follows the Harvard system (including how the same authors writing in the same year are differentiated using 'a' and 'b'). The use of 'et al.' (sometimes shown in italics), literally 'and others', denotes that more than two authors are involved (but all authors are reported in the reference list). Something approaching this style of academic writing will probably be expected of you in your own project.

Referencing work

It is absolutely essential that as you find more and more literature that you organise and manage it well. This applies across the individual research project as a whole and not just to the literature review. Simply citing authors in the main body of text is not enough, you have to compile a reference list too. So, right from the outset, record the details of everything you read accurately, even if not everything you find and read makes it into what you submit (see the worked example presented here). Keeping a list of references as you go can be a tedious part of the overall research process but an important one nevertheless. There are several reasons for keeping a good record of what you read.

- It is conventional to support your review of literature with reference to the work of others and to acknowledge their contribution as appropriate.

- It demonstrates that you have actually consulted credible academic sources of information and therefore read something worthwhile and meaningful.

- Your supervisor or other readers may wish to access the sources you have used out of interest or even to check the accuracy of your reporting and full details are required.

- Deciding that you need to go back to something you read a fortnight earlier but can't remember the details is a chore.

- It helps to avoid inadvertently plagiarising the work of others.

The Harvard Referencing System is perhaps the most common referencing system in use today and the system you will most likely be required to adopt. The Harvard System is an internationally recognised system based on the author or authors of a piece of work and the date it was published. It has the advantage of being easy to use and all references appear in one list in alphabetical order right at the end of a piece of work regardless of the type of source (e.g. journal article, textbook, website). Despite being *standardised*, you will find that there is some variation in style within the Harvard System. Just look at the reference lists attached to a few articles in journals or textbooks in the library or online to experience this first hand. Don't worry too much about this. While style may vary slightly, the principles attached to referencing do not. For journal articles, textbooks and websites, the following formats and examples would generally be considered acceptable:

- journal articles – author surname and initials, year of publication (in round brackets), title of article (sometimes in single quotation marks), title of journal (sometimes in italics or underlined), volume number (sometimes in bold), issue number (in round brackets) and page details;

- textbooks – author surname and initials, year of publication (in round brackets), title of book (sometimes in italics or underlined), place of publication, publishing company;

- websites – author surname and initials (or organisation), year of publication (in round brackets), title of website (sometimes in single quotation marks), website address (sometimes in italics or underlined), date accessed (in square brackets).

Crook, D. (2002) Education studies and teacher education. *British Journal of Education Studies*, 50(1): 57–75.

Hayes, D. (2004) *Foundations of primary teaching*. London: David Fulton.

Qualifications and Curriculum Authority (2008) *National Curriculum*. Available at: http://curriculum.qca.org.uk [accessed 1 July 2008].

If a textbook is edited or you acknowledge a chapter from within an edited textbook, adjust the formatting accordingly. Things also gets a little more complicated when journal articles and textbooks are accessed electronically but all you need to do is add [online] after the title of the journal or the title of the textbook.

Goouch, K. (2008) Understanding playful pedagogies, play narratives and play spaces. *Early Years* [online], 28(1): 93–102.

Sewell, K. and Newman, S. (2006) What is education? In: J. Sharp, S. Ward and L. Hankin (eds) *Education Studies: an issues-based approach*. Exeter: Learning Matters. 5–19.

Ward, S. (ed) (2004) *Education studies: a student's guide*. London: RoutledgeFalmer.

Avoid placing full website addresses in the main body of the text (it looks clumsy) and do not number or bullet-point references or insert them as footnotes unless specifically required to do so. Your own library or course handbook will almost certainly provide details of the Harvard style you should adopt in detail.

Summary of key points

Read widely, at least initially, and make sure you access the most recent journal articles, textbooks and websites in equal measure or as appropriate.

Your library really is your best friend. It's been said several times now, so it must be true.

Take care to ensure that the websites you look at via the internet are credible and reliable sources of information.

Use the research literature available to you to inform your work and to demonstrate that you are capable of reading and writing reflectively, critically and analytically as well as descriptively.

Develop strategies for effective note taking, reading and writing.

Keep a formal record of all of the sources of information you consult using the Harvard System or as directed by your own course handbook.

Make every effort to avoid copyright infringements and plagiarism.

Further reading

Hart (1998) provides a particularly detailed but readable account of the literature review which is now widely regarded as a classic text. Cottrell (2005) and Richardson and McBryde-Wilding (2009) together provide practical tips and hints with examples of how to find and use information accurately.

Cottrell, S. (2005) *Critical thinking skills: developing effective analysis and argument*. Basingstoke: Palgrave Macmillan.

Hart, C. (1998) *Doing a literature review: realising the social science imagination*. London: Sage.

Richardson, L. and McBryde-Wilding, H. (2009) *Information skills for education students*. Exeter: Learning Matters.

4. Approaching it in style

So far so good

So far you've settled on something worth investigating, come up with a working title and raised at least one provisional research question. You've started to look further into the research literature which is not only helping you to refine your focus but to get to grips with the literature review. You've worked everything up into a research proposal, outlined a general structure and plan, perhaps given some thought to how you might collect and analyse your data, and shared all of this with your supervisor. Your individual research project looks to be shaping up. Surely all you have to do now is get on and do it. But have you considered approaching your research in style? While educational research can be approached in any number of different ways, a small number of particular approaches have emerged as favoured over others and these offer guidance and support in terms of which style of research might be most suitable. Sometimes it may be possible to choose which approach you'd prefer right from the outset, particularly if you have a clear idea about what you want to do and how you want to do it. It may be that you have been directed towards one particular approach as a course requirement and have no choice at all. Often, however, you'll only get around to thinking about an approach as your knowledge of educational research grows and once some of the more basic aspects of your individual research project are in place. You'll certainly know when the time is right when asked about the *kind* or *type* of research you're doing by your supervisor. Some of the more common approaches currently in favour in education include:

- survey research;

- experimental research;

- case study research;

- action research;

- documentary research;

- ethnographic research;

- phenomenological research;

- grounded theory research.

The likelihood is that your work, either by design or by accident, will naturally align itself with one of the first five and more common of these whether it is classroom-based and attached to a placement or not. The remaining three are more involved and require far more time than you'll probably have available to you and are perhaps best avoided. It may turn out that what you want to do doesn't match any of the more common approaches at all or that making them fit just makes everything seem too contrived. That's fine. It's just as easy to take a more general approach and describe your research as:

- historical;

- developmental;

- exploratory;

- comparative;

- analytical.

What you can't do, however, is call it just descriptive or reflective. In educational research, and when studying education or training to be a teacher for the first time, description and reflection are pretty much taken for granted as a basic expectation. But if it doesn't matter if your project can be identified with any one particular approach or not then why bother with it at all? Aligning your work with a recognised approach carries certain benefits.

- It can provide a philosophical and theoretical framework within which your work can be located and contextualised.

- It can help make certain decisions concerning the overall design of your project by simply following accepted convention and practice (thereby minimising risk).

- It can help make more sense of the research literature and the language used to describe educational research.

It's also useful to just have that breadth of research knowledge at your fingertips. On the business of philosophical framework, certain approaches are often written about as falling under the umbrella of one or other of the two major research paradigms presented earlier, largely because of the sorts of knowledge they generate and how it's generated. Indeed, simply by selecting one approach over another you can, intentionally or unintentionally, send certain signals to your reader about your own research values and beliefs whether true and interpreted correctly or not.

Neither the boundaries between particular research paradigms nor the boundaries between different research approaches are quite so clearly defined, however, and while you should be aware of such associations you do not need to worry about them much at all. It is also important to note that no individual research approach presupposes the use of any one particular research method (e.g. questionnaire, interview, observation, use of documents) or means of data analysis (quantitative or qualitative) though some are often more strongly linked than others (e.g. surveys with questionnaires, case studies with interviews or observation). Indeed, the use of more than one method with any particular approach brings with it the opportunity to triangulate (to cross-reference, reduce ambiguity and increase confidence in findings) thus helping to ensure validity and reliability (whether or not the answer to your question or solution to your problem is credible, accurate and dependable). As you may already have noticed, there can be some confusion as to whether or not using documents constitutes an approach or a method for collecting data. Here, documentary research will be explored more fully alongside using questionnaires, interviews and observations.

Normative paradigm		Interpretive paradigm
Survey research		Case study research
	Documentary research	
Experimental research		Action research

Figure 4.1 Approaches and paradigms: common if not absolute associations

Practical task

Horses for courses

Once you've finished reading this chapter in full, consider each of the following working titles in turn and consider which, if any, approach you would adopt in order to proceed.

- Teachers' attitudes towards children with special educational needs.

- Children's role models and how they are perceived.

Practical task continued

- What children aspire to be as adults.

- Guided versus free reading and the National Literacy Strategy.

- Using writing journals.

- Oral and mental work in the National Numeracy Strategy.

- Computer use at home.

- Designing a new school playground.

- Gender effects on play in nursery classrooms.

- The Reggio Emilia environment.

- Practical work in science investigations.

- Gifted and talented children as learners.

- The value and effectiveness of circle time.

Can you begin to see that things are never quite that simple? What other information do you really need in order to proceed? How do you plan to approach your own individual research project?

Survey research

Survey research in education is often portrayed as requiring masses of data collected from masses of people which is then subjected to rigorous statistical analysis. While large-scale surveys certainly carry advantages in terms of their size and what they set out to achieve, surveys in education can be small-scale too and these make ideal individual research projects. Because of its very nature, small-scale survey research in education lends itself particularly well to:

- providing an overview of factual information about people, places or events as well as establishing any possible relationships that exist between them;

- exploring the views, opinions, perceptions, attitudes, preferences and behaviours among people and looking for possible explanations to account for them;

- using records of past surveys in order to describe and interpret possible patterns or trends or to make comparisons.

While there are many different ways of carrying out a survey, data collection usually involves a questionnaire. The different types of common survey include:

- the clipboard survey (questionnaire completed face-to-face during a meeting or interview with you);

- the telephone survey (questionnaire completed over the telephone);

- the self-completion survey (questionnaire distributed by hand, post, email or internet and completed by the respondent in his or her own time).

The type of survey you ultimately choose to undertake can be influenced by a number of factors including exactly what your survey is about, the questions you need to ask, the clarity and level of detail required, the access you have to potential respondents, the time you have available to you, and cost. The response rate for questionnaire surveys is particularly important and this is something you need to give very careful thought to. The response rate can be high if your work is classroom-based and you find yourself in direct contact with those you wish to work with (e.g. the face-to-face survey) but the response rate may drop off dramatically the more removed you become (e.g. the self-completion survey). Despite the appeal of postal, email and internet surveys, the response rate can be fatal. As a rule of thumb, always assume the worst and that you will only get back about 20 per cent of what you distribute and that not all of that may be usable. Anything more is a bonus.

Because of the diversity of work which counts as survey research, it is difficult to provide a single definition which fits every particular instance. What makes a survey a survey, however, is the business of identifying a target population of interest and sampling it accordingly. A target population is best thought of as the complete set of people, places or events of interest to you about which you wish to generalise. It's usually impossible to include every member of a target population in a survey and so you have to draw the best possible sample from it you can in the hope that findings adequately represent the target population as a whole. With small-scale surveys, your findings may be only representative of a more *local* target population (e.g. the children or teachers in any one school). You will not be able to extend your findings much beyond the confines of the individual research project itself and any attempt to generalise further would be unwise (e.g. to all children or teachers in all schools). Sampling is important to all forms of research not only to surveys and you need to be aware of the sampling limitations involved. Sampling strategies associated with surveys fall into two camps, probability sampling and non-probability sampling. Probability sampling is usually preferred if your sample size is likely to be quite generous. Strategies include:

- random sampling (e.g. selecting children entirely at random from a number of different schools);

- systematic sampling (e.g. selecting every n^{th} child from the class registers of a number of different schools);

- stratified random sampling (e.g. selecting the same proportion of children entirely at random from a number of different schools);

- cluster sampling (e.g. selecting children entirely at random from a cluster of *typical* schools in one geographical region).

Non-probability sampling is usually preferred if your sample size is likely to be less generous or if sample bias is not considered so much of a problem. Strategies include:

- opportunity sampling (e.g. selecting children from your own placement school);

- purposive or judgemental sampling (e.g. selecting children by handpicking those you wish to include from your own placement school);

- volunteer sampling (e.g. selecting children by allowing those in your own placement school to come forward themselves);

- snowball sampling (e.g. selecting children referred to you by other children in your own placement school).

The notion of what constitutes an appropriate sample size always causes confusion. It is often assumed that the larger the sample size the better the survey. The quality of your survey, as with all research, however, is determined by how well designed it is. There will always come a point of diminishing returns, of course, where additional responses lend nothing further to the survey itself. But poor data is poor data, no matter how much of it you have.

Reflective task

Surveys and sampling

There are some large-scale surveys you should be aware of. A useful short-list might include the following.

- The National Cohort studies based at the Centre for Longitudinal Studies (www.cls.ioe.ac.uk) and the Youth Cohort Study of teenagers in England and Wales which can be accessed via the Department for Children, Schools and Families (www.dcsf.gov.uk).

- The Progress in International Reading and Literacy Study (PIRLS) available via the National Foundation for Educational Research (www.nfer.ac.uk), the Trends in International Mathematics and Science Study (TIMSS at http://nces.ed.gov/timss) and the Programme for International Student Assessment (PISA at www.pisa.oecd.org).

These are important sites and they contain a wealth of potentially useful educational survey information. Browse the sites to get a feel for what large-scale surveys look like and how they're designed.

Survey research in education doesn't need to be large-scale or complicated. It can be used to answer quite functional questions (e.g. How do children and teachers travel to school? or How do people make use of outdoor centres, museums and galleries?) or even prove more penetrating (e.g. Children's attitudes towards . . ., Teachers' perceptions of . . ., Parents' views about . . .). Obtain a copy of the following article (print or online) and read it carefully paying particular attention to the authors' approach.

- Blatchford, P. and Sumpner, C. (1998) What do we know about breaktime? Results from a national survey of breaktime and lunchtime in primary and secondary schools. *British Educational Research Journal*, 24(1): 79–94.

This article reports findings from a questionnaire survey concerning itself with the positive and negative views of daily breaktimes obtained from staff in 1245 primary and 300 secondary schools in England. While this work is large scale, it serves to illustrate how you might find something in the research literature that you could work with and modify for your own individual research project (assuming your course allows you to do this). How might you take this research and apply it to a single school, perhaps the school you are about to work in on placement? With specific reference to methodology, including sampling, what could you keep the same and what might you need to change? Which sampling strategy do you think you would be able to use in a typical placement school? Is it possible to *reassemble* the actual questionnaire used by the authors? Do you think a study like this would make a valuable individual research project?

The procedures associated with survey research are generally quite straightforward.

- Establish exactly what it is you intend to survey, who will be involved and whether or not you need permission or access in order to carry out the work.

- Define your target population carefully, identify the survey type and sampling strategy best suited to what you want to do and consider how best to maximise response rate.

- Consider data collection carefully and the method or methods you need to employ.

- Carry out the survey adopting a strictly ethical approach at all times but especially if the subject matter might be considered sensitive or intrusive.

The real strength of survey research in education for you lies in its flexibility, breadth and scope and the potential to gather lots of data from even a small number of participants. It can also generate the sorts of findings that might be of very great interest and importance *locally*. On the other hand, undertaking a survey as part of an individual research project needs to be handled with care. Small-scale surveys may lack sufficient depth with which to really explore matters of interest in detail. There may be sampling issues to consider and sampling bias is always something to be aware of. Responses can be influenced by the age, gender, social class and ethnicity of respondents and, if working in a school or other educational organisation, by role, responsibility, experience, qualifications and training. You can never be entirely certain about what motivates people to respond or not or that people are being entirely honest in what they have to say when they do.

Experiments

Experimental research in education is not as common as it once was. It still goes on, of course, and it still has a place in terms of what it sets out to achieve. It's perfectly possible for you to carry out an experiment for your individual research project provided you can locate willing participants and that you can overcome any ethical obstacles in the way. Teachers and other educators *experiment* all the time, of course, but not in the formal way that you'd expect to find experiments conducted in a laboratory by scientists. Pure experimental research in education is virtually impossible because you just can't set up the experiment to be as *clinical* as you might like and you can't always isolate and control every possible variable or other factor that might have a bearing on outcome. Even if you could do all of these things there's nothing you can do about the matter of *free will* among participants and the unpredictability of human behaviour. For these reasons and more, educational experiments are often referred to as field experiments, the term *field* referring to any classroom-based environment other than a laboratory. Accepting that the classroom is a little more messy and untidy than the scientific laboratory, and that asking questions and solving problems really is as valid as testing hypotheses, educational experiments come into their own when you might be interested in attempting to evaluate or measure in relative or absolute terms:

- the cause-effect relationships particularly associated with teaching and learning;

- the effectiveness of different teaching strategies and how they compare.

There are a great many experimental designs available to choose from but the three most common include:

- the pre-experimental design;

- the quasi-experimental design;

- the true experimental design.

The pre-experimental design (also referred to as the one group pre-test/post-test design) is the simplest and the one most likely to be available to you. Suppose, for example, that you are looking to determine the impact of a new series of television programmes aimed at what it means to be a good citizen and which focus on the attitude of children towards healthy eating in one class in one school. In experimental research, the class of children becomes the *experimental group*, the series of television programmes the *intervention* or *experimental treatment*, *healthy eating* the independent variable (what you choose to isolate from within good citizenship and can manipulate in the sense that you can decide what to include or not) and *attitude* the dependent variable (a change in which depends on the impact of the television series and how healthy eating is portrayed within it). The language of experimentation is enough to put anyone off. You, as the researcher, could then set out to observe the attitude of each and every individual in the experimental group immediately before exposing them to the *experimental treatment* (usually denoted O_1) and again soon afterwards (usually denoted O_2). Traditionally, the term *observe* would normally be taken to mean *test* thus allowing for numerical measurement (hence pre-test/post-test). These days, however, testing in the conventional sense is not at all necessary and data collection by any appropriate means, including the use of questionnaires and interviews, is acceptable. The impact of the television programmes in relation to the independent variable can then be evaluated by considering any changes in attitude which take place (e.g. considering what was observed at O_2 in relation to O_1 or if numerical measurements were involved $O_2 - O_1$). The pre-experimental design is often simplified and represented as follows:

Experiment group	O_1	X	O_2

Figure 4.2 **Pre-experimental design**

You may have worked out by now, of course, that it would be very difficult, no matter how tempting, for you to attribute any change in attitude towards healthy eating entirely to the series of television programmes itself. Any number of unknown factors or extraneous variables may have contributed, either at school, at home or elsewhere. You could never be sure that the experimental treatment was the only thing to influence the outcome. This lack of control warrants the term *pre-experimental*.

The quasi-experimental design (also referred to as the pre-test/post-test non-equivalent control group design) can help overcome some of the pre-experimental shortcomings and this is often simplified and represented as follows:

Experiment group	O_1	X	O_2
Control group	O_3		O_4

Figure 4.3 **Quasi-experimental design**

The quasi-experimental design is better because it involves another group, the control group, against which changes in the experimental group can be compared (e.g. considering not only what was observed at O_2 in relation to O_1 but also O_4 in relation to O_3 or if numerical measurements were involved $O_2 - O_1$ in relation to $O_4 - O_3$). The use of a control group helps to eliminate the effect of some extraneous variables even if these cannot be fully identified. In a school or other classroom-based environment, the control group might be another class of children of much the same age and with similar background characteristics (hence the term *non-equivalent*). Establishing how well matched in age and background characteristics a control group might be can be a lengthy process but an essential one if you are ever to evaluate whether or not the experimental treatment had any real impact at all. Taking the healthy eating example further, the impact and effectiveness of using the new series of television programmes with the experimental group could be compared directly to the school's existing citizenship education provision or not as the case may be. In true experimental designs, all participants are placed within the experimental and control groups entirely at random rather than by opportunity. This and other requirements make true educational experiments difficult to undertake.

Reflective task

The place of experimentation

Experimentation is very definitely not as popular in education as it once was and there are few really good, readily accessible accounts available. Obtain a copy of the following article (print or online) and read it carefully paying particular attention to the authors' approach:

- Sharp, J.G. and Kuerbis, P. (2005) Children's ideas about the solar system and the chaos in learning science. *Science Education*, 90(1): 124–147.

This article presents details of a small-scale quasi-experimental study carried out with 31 primary-aged children in each of two classes (the experimental and control groups). It's all a bit technical in places but persevere. Can you identify the *experimental group*, *control group*, *experimental treatment*, *independent variable* and *dependent variable*? What extraneous variables just cannot be accounted for in any experiment of this type and how might they cast doubt on outcomes? Why was some degree of control very important? Do you think the authors managed to retain something of the *naturalness* of the classroom thus establishing what is often referred to as *ecological validity*? To what extent might these findings be generalised and considered representative of children in other classrooms?

In recent years there appears to have been a move towards relaxing the language and rigour surrounding educational experimentation towards a more user-friendly and evaluative approach. Such *design experiments* have great scope and potential for exploring the processes involved in experimentation, the behaviours of those participating and the meanings behind outcomes rather than just the outcomes themselves. This perhaps makes experimentation more appealing either on its own or used in association with other research approaches. Search for more about *design experiments*. Obtain a copy of the following article (print or online) and read its defence of experimentation:

- Marsden, E. (2007) Can educational experiments both test a theory and inform practice? *British Educational Research Journal*, 33(4): 565–588.

This article really is quite technical but if experimentation is your thing you should work through it (it's a useful source for related articles at the very least). How do you feel about the place of experimentation in education as a result? Do you think the criticisms often levelled at experimental research are justified?

The basic procedures attached to educational experiments are outlined as follows.

- Establish exactly what your experiment is about, which type of experimental design is best suited to your circumstance, who will be involved and whether or not you need permission or access in order to carry out the work.

- Identify the experimental group, the control group if required, the independent and dependent variables and describe the intervention or experimental treatment in detail.

- Consider data collection carefully and the method or methods you need to employ.

- Carry out the experiment adopting a strictly ethical approach at all times but especially if the subject matter is sensitive or intrusive (experimental research in education can be particularly sensitive ethically and you may need to obtain additional permission from an ethics committee well in advance even if you have already found willing participants).

Small-scale experimental research has strengths particularly in terms of the rigour with which it is conducted. In the best of circumstances, findings might be considered objective, unequivocal and repeatable under the same experimental conditions. On the other hand, educational experiments can be difficult to organise and manage and not all extraneous variables are easy to identify or account for. You can never even be sure that a positive intervention or treatment will be long lasting. Design experiments may offer more potential in terms of understanding the processes involved in experimentation itself, the behaviours of those taking part and the meanings behind outcomes rather than the outcomes themselves. As such, they might also usefully inform practice. Ethically, it might be argued that participants in control groups are treated unfairly and unnecessarily disadvantaged or that they may feel left out and demoralised. Claims and counter-claims abound.

Case studies

Case study research in education also concerns itself with people, places and events but differs from survey research by taking an interest in the functioning of *wholes* rather than *parts*. The *case* in a case study is usually taken to be a self-contained and coherent unit of analysis with clear and well defined boundaries in terms of participants, location, organisation, time and context or a combination of these. Examples might include an individual child or teacher, a class of children, an entire year group, a department, a school, an outdoor centre, a museum or a gallery. With an effective sample size of one (though several cases can be studies together), case study research has the potential to provide you with a level of detail unattainable by any other means. Case study research lends itself particularly well to:

- observing, describing, analysing and interpreting the behaviours of *real people* in *real settings* and the relationships and interactions that exist between them (even if the *case* happens to be an individual);

- exploring the subtleties and intricacies of complex situations surrounding existing conditions and cultures within organisations without interfering with or manipulating them;

- providing detailed narrative and chronological accounts or stories of how *real people* in *real settings* co-exist and which may provide the basis for comparison.

Case study research, then, is often more about the dynamics of everyday life rather than the outcomes or products which emerge as a result of it (e.g. actions, activities, decisions, judgements, change). In terms of selection, it is important that any *case* you settle upon has characteristic features of interest worthy of in-depth investigation and reporting. The way in which you sample is therefore usually by choice rather than by any other pre-determined sampling strategy. Extreme or unusual *cases* are perfectly acceptable. The child study is a particularly popular individual research project topic. Child studies are undertaken on the basis that teachers and other educators should be keen observers of those they work most closely with and that to see the world through their eyes helps to understand the complex lives they lead and how they view the system within which they are placed. Within any one particular child study, it is important to try to focus on the whole child, incorporating elements of his or her cognitive, linguistic, social, emotional and physical development, and how, if at school, learning is being supported. The narrative and chronological accounts or stories which emerge from a typical child study can be both alive and rich. While observation may be the main means of data collection, as it might be with a child study for example, case study research may also involve the use of supplementary questionnaires, interviews and documentary research.

(Reflective task)

Putting the *case* in case study

Individual research projects often develop into case studies but deciding what the *case* in question should be is not always straightforward. The *case* in a case study is usually taken to be a self-contained and coherent unit of analysis with clear and well defined boundaries in terms of participants, location, organisation, time and context or a combination of these and that the characteristic features of the *case* should be worthy of investigation and reporting. Meeting these criteria is not always easy. Obtain a copy of the following article (print or online) and read it carefully paying particular attention to the author's approach:

* Wall, K. (2004) The National Literacy Strategy and setting: an investigation in one school. *The Curriculum Journal*, 15(3): 233–246.

This article essentially concerns itself with the issue of setting or ability grouping as a means of organising and delivering the literacy hour in one junior school from the perspectives of the teachers, the children and the researcher herself who taught there. Does the author establish what the *case* is in terms of a unit of analysis and boundaries to your satisfaction? Has the author accounted for reflexivity? What do you think a single *case* like this one has to offer in the terms of the conclusions presented by the author?

Reflect on your recent experiences of education as a whole and the different educational environments you've found yourself in. You might even give some thought to the one you are in now. Can you think of any suitable *cases* that would make good project material? How would you define their boundaries and characteristic features? How would you organise the research and what would you do to minimise the *researcher effect* of having you around as the observer? How would you *feel* and *react* over time if you were knowingly the *object* of special attention? What impact might all of this have on the data you collect and its value?

With case study research, the following procedures are usually considered essential.

* Establish exactly what your case study is about, who or what will be involved and whether or not you need permission or access in order to carry out the work.

* Select your *case* carefully, clearly outlining its boundaries, and consider the characteristic features of the *case* which give your research its purpose and distinctiveness.

* Consider data collection carefully and the method or methods you need to employ.

* Carry out the research adopting a strictly ethical approach at all times but especially if the subject matter of your case study is sensitive.

The real strength of case study research lies in it being relatively easy to do. It has the potential to provide lots of data collected in a variety of different ways. If your individual research project happens to be classroom-based, the choice of potential *cases* is almost endless provided that you can demonstrate having met the criteria for identifying and selecting a *case* in the first instance. On the other hand, defining the boundaries of a *case* or justifying its characteristic features is not always so easy for these can be nebulous to say the least. When coming to write up a case study, the narrative and chronological accounts or stories you produce must be analytical and based upon evidence and not just descriptive or tending towards anecdote. Case study research also places you at the heart of the research process as a *player*. Your own involvement, even as an observer, may have a profound impact on what those around you say and do and so reflexivity must be accounted for in full.

Action research

The term *action research*, or *educational action research* to give it its full title, has come to mean different things to different people. In general terms, however, action research in education might best be thought of as the sort of research undertaken by teachers and other educators themselves, either individually, collectively or working very closely with an external researcher, in order to find answers to questions and solutions to problems that they ask and face at work every day and which address specific issues, needs and concerns. Conducted carefully and with rigour, action research is intended to lead to improvements in the effectiveness of practice by generating *knowledge-for-action*. Action research might also be considered synonymous with practitioner research though practitioner research is perhaps less attached to some of the more defining characteristics of what is referred to as the action research cycle. Action research is particularly intended to help teachers and other educators:

- understand and learn from the everyday situations they find themselves in and which require attention;

- challenge for themselves and bring about change and improvements in what they do and the conditions under which they do it;

- take ownership of and responsibility for their own practice and justify their actions;

- continue to develop professionally.

As a result, action research lends itself particularly well to investigating almost any aspect of professional activity in almost any educational environment using almost any means of data collection available (though observation with support from questionnaires and interviews is often preferred). Action research, then, is highly contextualised within the world of work and undertaken with the benefit of *insider knowledge* and an acute awareness of what matters most. If undertaking action research, you might find yourself considering a question, problem, issue, concern or need of your own or working alongside a teacher or other educator helping with something of theirs.

At the heart of action research, and what distinguishes it from how you might go about tackling the unforeseen situations thrown at you during the course of a normal working day, lies a commitment to critical and analytical enquiry and the ability to implement, monitor, evaluate and reflect upon what you find. Action research is, therefore, something of an ongoing, formative, proactive and evolutionary process. This is recognised in the procedures attached to it.

- Establish exactly what your action research is about, who will be involved and whether or not you need permission or access in order to carry out the work.

- Clearly identify with supporting evidence what needs to be addressed in terms of how it impacts on your own professional practice.

- Reflect upon current practice critically and analytically and consider appropriate and alternative solutions or courses of action with suitable success criteria against which outcomes might be evaluated.

- Implement solutions or courses of action, monitor change and evaluate effectiveness against success criteria (considering data collection carefully and the method or methods you need to employ).

- Reflect upon change critically and analytically, adjust and modify action accordingly and repeat until addressed to your satisfaction.

- Adopt a strictly ethical approach at all times but especially if the subject matter of your action research is sensitive or intrusive.

Such procedures are often presented as forming something of an action research cycle and it is the cyclical nature of action research that underpins the notion of continuing professional development.

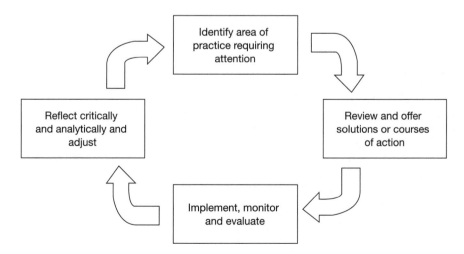

Figure 4.4 **A simplified action research cycle**

(Reflective task)

Legitimising action research

Action research is certainly appealing for it would appear at first sight to be just the sort of research that everyone interested in education should be doing. What could be more important than improving practice? Suffice it to say that such a view might be considered a bit narrow to say the least and many who adhere to more traditional forms of enquiry might argue strongly that action research just lacks credibility. Obtain a copy of the following article (print or online) and read it carefully paying particular attention to the authors' approach and the approach adopted by the teachers involved:

* Bartlett, S. and Burton, D. (2006) A description of classroom practice? A discussion of teachers investigating their classrooms. *Educational Action Research*, 14(3): 395–405.

This article outlines how a small group of research networked teachers working in a cluster of nine different primary schools went about doing some action research collaboratively in order to improve the effectiveness of what they did in their own classrooms. The authors take this example as a *case* to illustrate how certain characteristic features of the action research process legitimise action research as a valid form of enquiry. Consider the evidence presented and make up your own mind. Do you think that research undertaken by practitioners themselves is any more or any less valid than research undertaken by anybody else? To be more accurate, the authors refer to the research undertaken as *practitioner* rather than action research. Are you clear about the difference between the two?

Give some thought to the sorts of professional questions or problems you've faced in the past. These might be to do with teaching and learning, assessment, organisation and management, administration, behaviour management, and so on. Could these have been addressed following the action research cycle? Follow the action research cycle outlined here to tease out some of the detail.

Perhaps the single greatest strength of educational action research (or practitioner research) is that it is carried out by teachers or other educators themselves in order to improve their own practice or the practice of others through the creation of *knowledge-for-action*. At times, however, action research may involve you having to work with others and so the ownership of the research and its outcomes may need to be carefully negotiated and established. Being located within the *workplace* may also place constraints on the nature of any possible research activity you can do, particularly if attached to a placement. Educational action research also locates you as a *player* in the research process in the same way that case study research does and reflexivity must be accounted for in full.

Summary of key points

If you set out with a specific approach in mind or you don't have a choice then read about it as much as you can. There is no substitute for this necessary groundwork. Find examples of studies which have followed a similar approach. They might offer up some valuable insights and help.

If the work you have in mind doesn't readily align itself with an existing approach or it seems to sit on the boundary between two or more approaches then don't worry. Sometimes that's just the way it is. Describe it accordingly. The principles underpinning all approaches are pretty much the same.

All approaches have their strengths and limitations, particularly in terms of the extent to which findings can be generalised and considered representative of the wider world of education. Consider your own work carefully and fully and resist the temptation to make claims you can't justify beyond the evidence you have and the confines of your research.

If your approach places you at the heart of the research process as a player, don't forget to consider and discuss reflexivity when you eventually write up.

Further reading

Within this longer than usual list, Denscombe (2007) provides perhaps the most valuable overview of research approaches. Cohen et al. (2007) is particularly good if you need to really explore approaches in considerable detail. A selection of older but classic sources are also presented which you might find useful. The approach is contained within the title.

Barnett, V. (2002) *Sample survey: principles and methods*. London: Hodder/Arnold.

Bassey, M. (1999) *Case study research in educational settings*. Milton Keynes: Open University Press.

Campbell, D.T. and Stanley, J.C. (1963) Experimental and quasi-experimental designs for research on teaching. In: N.L. Gage (ed) *Handbook of research on teaching*. Chicago: Rand McNally. 171–243.

Carr, W. and Kemmis, S. (1986) *Becoming critical: education, knowledge and action research*. Lewes: Falmer.

Cohen, L., Manion, L. and Morrison, K. (2007) *Research methods in education*. London: Routledge.

Denscombe, M. (2007) *The good research guide for small-scale social research projects*. Maidenhead: McGraw-Hill/Open University Press.

Elliott, J. (1991) *Action research for educational change*. Milton Keynes: Open University Press.

Kemmis, S. and McTaggart, R. (eds) (1992) *The action research planner*. Victoria: Deakin University Press.

McNiff, J. and Whitehead, J. (2002) *Action research: principles and practice*. London: Routledge.

Moser, C. and Kalton, G. (1971) *Survey methods in social investigation*. London: Heinemann.

Vause, D. (2002) *Surveys in social research*. London: Routledge.

Yin, R.K. (2002) *Case study research: design and methods*. London: Sage.

5. Discovering things: questionnaires

Learning outcomes

Questionnaires are valuable research tools. In the right hands, they provide a method for collecting all sorts of data from all sorts of different people about all sorts of different things. But questionnaires also have their drawbacks too. Design and construct them badly and what they provide can be pretty shallow and meaningless. By having read this chapter and completed the tasks within it, you will:

- know about the questionnaire as a research tool and as a method for collecting data;

- be able to design and construct your own questionnaire in accordance with conventional practice;

- be able to conduct a questionnaire survey with confidence;

- be aware of some of the strengths and limitations of questionnaires as used in educational research.

The questionnaire as a research tool

The questionnaire has been defined in its most basic sense as everything from a simple collection of pre-formulated questions to a means of discovering things. They crop up everywhere in everyday life. You can find them in newspapers and magazines. They arrive with the rest of the mail through your letterbox, and it's virtually impossible to walk from one end of the high street in any town or city to the other without someone trying to stop you to fill one in. You'll certainly be very familiar with completing questionnaires yourself as virtually everything you've done on your own course so far will probably have been evaluated using one. The questionnaire is particularly suited for use in survey research in education but may just as easily find itself included as part of almost any other approach either as the principal means of collecting data or for providing supplementary information for the purposes of clarification or triangulation. Questionnaires are commonly employed in individual research projects if the aim is:

- to collect straightforward information from any number of participants, large or small;

- to explore the prevalence of expressed views, opinions, perceptions, attitudes, preferences and behaviours;

- to achieve a relatively high level of standardisation without a requirement for personal interaction.

The questionnaire, then, is a particularly versatile and adaptable research tool.

Designing, constructing and using questionnaires

Questionnaires concern themselves with asking questions to which respondents provide answers (the clue in the name is a bit of a give away). That said, it is also possible to request responses to statements too. Having established that using a questionnaire is indeed the best method of getting the data you need in order to answer your research question or to solve your problem you can then begin to think about designing one. There may well be an *off the shelf* solution available to you, of course, particularly if you are setting out to replicate something already appearing in the research literature. But even if there is, time moves on. Ideas and circumstances change and researchers don't necessarily want to use the same questionnaire even if their intentions are very similar. In any event, the questionnaires used to collect data in any existing studies are unlikely to appear published in full in the original texts and you may find yourself having to piece them together from what is reported in the descriptions of method and findings. Be prepared to adapt and modify. There are three basic types of questionnaire, the designs for which vary accordingly.

- Structured – where the content and form of response is determined by the researcher using closed questions (these are easier to analyse and normally used when very large sample sizes are involved).

- Unstructured – where the content and form of response is determined by the respondent from open questions (these are harder to analyse and normally used when very small sample sizes are involved).

- Semi-structured – where the content and form of response is determined using a mixture of questions (these are well suited to individual research projects).

Structured questionnaires provide little means of obtaining clarification or further explanation from respondents even if you do happen to be present administering a questionnaire yourself. Using unstructured questionnaires requires experience and care if focus and direction are to be maintained. Semi-structured questionnaires offer up a sensible middle ground.

Questionnaires tend to use only two types of question, closed and open. Closed questions, which tend to be more common in most questionnaires, allow individuals to respond according to choices selected in advance by you and usually by ticking a box or circling a word (forced-choice). These are best used when the range of possible replies is limited in number and perhaps known in advance from piloting.

Closed questions can sometimes be scaled to allow numerical forms of measurement to take place. There are several commonly recognised forms of closed question and response mode available to choose from:

- dichotomous questions which require choosing only one from two possible responses (e.g. yes or no, male or female);

- category questions which require choosing only one response from a range of categories provided (e.g. teaching experience gathered together and presented in blocks of years);

- list questions which require choosing more than one response from a list of options provided (e.g. teaching qualifications);

- exact answer questions (e.g. the exact year in which a respondent qualified to teach);

- rank order questions which require words, phrases or sentences to be prioritised or ordered (e.g. words associated with the attraction of teaching as a career);

- rating or measure of agreement questions answered using a Likert-type scale (e.g. 1=strongly disagree to 5=strongly agree);

- semantic differential questions using opposing or bi-polar adjectives arranged in a grid with a scale of any size (e.g. this classroom is too cold- – – – – – – – – – too hot, too quiet- – – – – – – – – -too noisy).

Open questions allow individuals to respond in any way they choose (free-choice). Open questions are particularly suited to working face-to-face or where the matters being investigated are perhaps more complex and require elaboration. Even then, extracting meaning can still prove difficult. Open questions are also useful during piloting, particularly if looking to produce more focused closed questions which can be handled more readily during analysis. Closed or open, try to start with easier or less threatening questions first to lead respondents gently in before moving on to the main thrust of your work.

Because questionnaires are often associated with survey research (though not exclusively by any means), they are usually administered in one of three ways.

- By clipboard (questionnaire completed face-to-face).

- By telephone (questionnaire completed by telephone).

- By self-completion (questionnaire distributed by hand, by post, by email or by internet and completed by the respondent in their own time).

Regardless of how you administer a questionnaire, always ensure that it includes a cover page outlining clearly the title of the study and its purpose, your own name and the course you are taking, a reminder near the end to check that all questions have been answered fully and accurately, return details if you will not be available to collect the questionnaire yourself immediately (incorporate a *complete by* date and supply a stamped and self-addressed envelope if postal) and a token of appreciation in the form of a thank you for the respondent's time. Take care over the visual appearance of a questionnaire by keeping it neat and tidy and never distribute poor photocopies. Above all, keep your questionnaire as short as possible. The longer it takes to complete, the less likely it will be that it comes back completed or in a usable state. Fortunately, a questionnaire provides its own record of outcomes and nothing else is usually required. Steps in the process of designing, constructing and using an interview schedule might be summarised as follows.

- Be clear about the nature and purpose of the data you need in relation to your research question or problem.

- Consider how many questions or items are necessary and the form and logical sequence these might take in order to probe effectively.

- Create a trial questionnaire and pilot and amend this accordingly paying particular attention to areas of concern raised in feedback.

- Distribute the questionnaires as required.

- Subject your data to an appropriate means of interrogation and analysis (usually leaning towards quantitative – though the qualitative analysis of questionnaire data is perfectly acceptable).

Worked example

Teachers and the national curriculum

The task

Jenny was a PGCE student with a particular interest in how prepared primary teachers felt to teach across all subject areas of the National Curriculum. She was also interested in their recent in-service histories and requirements. Jenny wanted to collect as much data as possible from teachers working in a number of different schools rather than just the school she was about to start her own placement in later (though she hoped to be able to interview the teachers there in more detail in the light of outcomes). She'd already approached her supervisor to find out if it might be possible to administer her questionnaire to the teachers invited to attend a forthcoming placement briefing. This request had been taken forward and approved. She would only have access to the teachers as a group for about 20 minutes before lunch. The nature and purpose of Jenny's project, together with the amount of time and opportunity available to her, almost dictated using a questionnaire. This was developed with full acknowledgement from similar questionnaires appearing in the research literature and through several drafts to reach the stage presented here. As you read through, focus your attention not on the completed questionnaire itself as such but on each and every individual item, how it has been designed and constructed, its role in sequence, and perhaps why Jenny presented it this way. Take particular notice of how Jenny starts by collecting simple demographic information first, leaving the main thrust of the questionnaire until later.

How prepared do you feel to teach the National Curriculum?

1. **Are you male or female?**

   male ☐
   female ☐

2. **Who are you?**

   head teacher ☐
   deputy head teacher ☐
   class teacher ☐
   other (specify e.g. classroom assistant) .... ☐

   (you may tick more than one box)

3. **How long have you been teaching?**

   enter in years ....

4. **What teaching qualification(s) do you currently hold?**

   Teaching certificate/diploma ☐
   BEd ☐
   BA/BSc in primary education ☐
   degree with PGCE (specify e.g. history) .... ☐
   other (specify e.g. NPQH, MEd, PhD) .... ☐

   (you may tick more than one box)

5. **Which curriculum area are you mainly responsible for across the school?**

   English ☐
   Mathematics ☐
   Science ☐
   Design and technology ☐
   ICT ☐
   History ☐
   Geography ☐
   Art and design ☐
   Music ☐
   Physical education ☐
   Religious education ☐
   other (specify e.g. SEN, PHSE, citizenship, none) .... ☐

6. **Which type of school do you work in?**

   infant ☐
   junior ☐
   primary ☐
   other (specify e.g. first, middle) .... ☐

7. Which year group(s) do you currently teach?

Reception ☐
Year 1 ☐
Year 2 ☐
Year 3 ☐
Year 4 ☐
Year 5 ☐
Year 6 ☐
other (specify e.g. mixed R/Y1, Y5/6) .... ☐

(you may tick more than one box)

8. How prepared do you feel to teach across the curriculum?

Please consider each curriculum area below using the criteria and scale provided (please tick one box per subject only):

5 = I feel very well prepared to teach this subject and would be happy to help others

4 = I feel sufficiently well prepared to teach this subject and know that I can always rely on a little in-service support

3 = I feel that I would be sufficiently well prepared to teach this subject with a little in-service support help from colleagues

2 = I do not feel sufficiently prepared to teach this subject at all and require substantial in-service support

1 = This is my weakest subject and even with substantial in-service support I may have a long way to go before I'll ever feel prepared

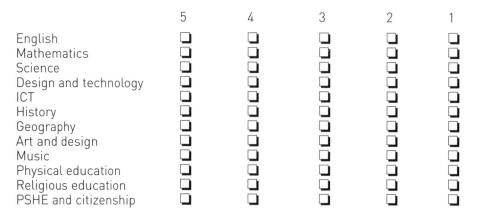

	5	4	3	2	1
English	☐	☐	☐	☐	☐
Mathematics	☐	☐	☐	☐	☐
Science	☐	☐	☐	☐	☐
Design and technology	☐	☐	☐	☐	☐
ICT	☐	☐	☐	☐	☐
History	☐	☐	☐	☐	☐
Geography	☐	☐	☐	☐	☐
Art and design	☐	☐	☐	☐	☐
Music	☐	☐	☐	☐	☐
Physical education	☐	☐	☐	☐	☐
Religious education	☐	☐	☐	☐	☐
PSHE and citizenship	☐	☐	☐	☐	☐

9. **Which single area of the curriculum from the list above do you most enjoy teaching?**

    Area? ....

    Why? ....

10. **Which single area of the curriculum from the list above do you least enjoy teaching?**

    Area? ....

    Why? ....

11. **Have you taken advantage of any in-service provision organised by your school within the past 3 years?**

    yes   ❑
    no   ❑

    Please provide details:

    ....

    ....

12. **To what extent do you agree with the following statement?**

    I have had every opportunity to participate in the in-service training organised by my Local Authority within the past three years (circle only one):

    Strongly agree   Agree   Neither agree   Disgree   Strongly disagree
                                           nor disagree

    Please provide details:

    ....

    ....

    [Please just take a moment to make sure that you have answered all of the questions fully and accurately. Thank you for your time and participation.]

Though basic in terms of what it will provide, you should be able to see how Jenny's 12-item questionnaire leads respondents from beginning to end with considerable ease. The form of the questions and statements seems entirely appropriate, a variety of response modes are incorporated and the sequence is about as good as it can be. You should also be able to determine why she chose the questions and statements she did and why they appear as they do. Jenny went on to be able to explore the data provided to good effect and to consider many possible relationships between individual items in detail. Could the questionnaire have been designed and constructed differently?

Things to be avoided

Pitfalls commonly associated with questionnaire design are presented as follows.

- Avoid ambiguous questions. How big is your class? Do you mean in square metres or the number of children on the register? OK, it's obvious in this example, but it's not always so easy.

- Avoid unfamiliar words and phrases and questions that presume a level of background knowledge. It all depends on who your questionnaire is aimed at but try to keep technical jargon to a minimum at all times unless you are absolutely certain that your respondents are sufficiently informed to be able to answer in a meaningful way.

- Avoid vague terms and long and over-elaborate questions. Terms such as *often*, *kind of* and *sort of* clog up the clarity of a questionnaire and introduce unwanted ambiguities. How often do you have a school lunch? What does *often* mean? Be more precise. Long and over-elaborate questions simply take time to read and may confuse.

- Avoid leading or loaded questions. These produce biased, distorted and inaccurate outcomes. Should all state schools receive more government funding in order to support learners more effectively? You can see the problem. Questions like this may appear by accident but they may also appear because you are looking to provoke a response which supports your own position.

- Avoid asking more than one question at a time. Which school clubs does your child participate in and which other clubs do they attend during evenings or at weekends? Use two or more questions if necessary.

- Avoid hypothetical questions. If you were the class teacher . . . ? You're not so why ask? Unless you're looking for a wish list don't bother.

- Avoid negatives (single, double or more). These just make questions hard to understand and could lead to incorrect responses. To what extent do you agree or disagree with the line *We don't need no education?*

- Avoid sensitive or intrusive questions. Sometimes even the simplest request for information falls into this category. Enquiring directly about the socio-economic background of a parent or carer or who gets a free meal can raise eyebrows. Do you really need to know?

- Avoid questions that require recall over an unreasonable amount of time. As a teacher, how did you feel about the National Curriculum when it was first launched in 1989? Don't be surprise if some of your respondents were still attending school as a pupil themselves.

Reflective task

The devil in the detail

Using questionnaires is not always appropriate. While questionnaires can prove useful for collecting straightforward information from any number of participants, large or small, it is essential that you are clear about the nature and purpose of the data you need in relation to your research question or problem. Obtain a copy of the following article (print or online):

- Lambert, M. (2008) Devil in the detail: using a pupil questionnaire survey in an evaluation of out-of-school classes for gifted and talented children. *Education 3–13*, 36(1): 69–78.

The article concerns itself with a national evaluation of out-of-school classes provided by *advanced learning centres* attended by very able primary-aged children. This is a particularly useful article for it conveys something of the challenges faced in using questionnaires by at least one author and brings into focus the importance of design, interpretation, sources of bias and ethics. Read the article carefully teasing out and reflecting upon the pros and cons of using questionnaires as described. To what extent do you agree or not with the position presented? Do you think any other method of data collection (e.g. interview, observation, using documents) would be any more productive?

Working with children

Designing and constructing a questionnaire for use by children will inevitably be influenced by a wide range of factors including age, reading ability, interest, perseverance and the ability to articulate a valid and reliable response. There are questionnaires available which have been used successfully with children as young as 5 but the extent to which a questionnaire can be completed independently by children this young or even younger is not at all clear. You or others may need to get involved to help and the impact of this, if any, needs to be carefully considered. In essence, questionnaires for children should be shorter, simpler and perhaps more attractively set out and appealing than those for adults. A narrower range of response modes should be considered and conventional Likert-type scales (e.g. 1=strongly disagree to 5=strongly agree) might be replaced with sad and smiley faces or similar expressions on the faces of popular cartoon characters. Piloting in advance is essential.

I disagree   I agree

Figure 5.1 **An alternative Likert-type scale**

If you're on placement in a school, you may have the luxury of being able to choose how best to administer your questionnaires (e.g. face-to-face with individuals, with groups or with a whole class). If elsewhere (e.g. an outdoor centre, a museum or a gallery), you may have to take any opportunity that arises so be prepared and plan accordingly. Always make sure that those in authority in a school or elsewhere know what you are doing and that you have obtained permission.

Practical task

Children's attitudes towards reading

Finding questionnaires for use by children is relatively easy, particularly if searching using the internet. Not all questionnaires found in this way are of any use when it comes to research, however, so make sure you've earned your stripes as an *Internet Detective* in advance and don't forget to acknowledge your sources fully (see Chapter 3). Here, you are presented with 15 questions and statements from a few different internet sources which could be reworked with a little thought into a valuable reading attitude questionnaire. Begin by placing the questions and statements in a better order than they are in right now then adapt and modify the form of any you think require attention. Try to include as wide a range of different response modes as possible.

- Reading is pointless, important, boring, fun, easy, hard, for boys, for girls, stressful, relaxing.

- Do you like to receive books as presents?

- I am in Year __ at school.

- Do you like reading to others?

- Are you a good reader?

- I am __ years and __ months old.

- I like to read at home, at a friend's house, in the local library, at school.

- Do you like reading by yourself?

- I am encouraged to read at home.

- My favourite book is __ and I like it because __.

- I am a boy/girl.

- Reading makes me feel calm, excited, happy, sad, stupid, clever.

- I find reading difficult.

- Which book are you reading at the moment __ .

- I like reading story books, information books, picture books, hobby books, comics, annuals, poems, joke books.

Give some thought to what your final questionnaire might look like if designed for infants, juniors or even older pupils. If you were looking to investigate attitude to reading as part of your own individual research project, which questions (or statements) would you keep and which would you reject? Can you think of others you'd include? Now try preparing some questionnaires on topics of your own. Pilot the questionnaires with others on your own course and consider the feedback they provide.

Strengths and limitations

Questionnaires provide the opportunity to collect straightforward information in a fairly standardised way with relatively little effort and with few adverse effects involving you as the researcher. As indicated earlier, however, questionnaires can be rendered pretty much useless if thoughtlessly and carelessly designed and constructed in the first place or, for that matter, thoughtlessly and carelessly completed by respondents. Questionnaires take time to fill in, of course, and this can be off-putting particularly for busy people. The extent to which closed questions and different response modes shape outcomes and introduce bias is certainly something which needs to be considered carefully and box ticking can never quite capture anything of the complexity of people's lives or the contexts in which they operate. Many respondents may be left feeling frustrated at not being able to express themselves more openly and fully and the interpretation of meaning from the data made available can be problematic as a result. Even existing questionnaires which may look useful and which you may wish to borrow, acknowledge and use can lack sufficient content or fail to really live up to expectation in terms of what they claim to be able to do. Establishing the validity and reliability of any questionnaire, including a questionnaire you design and construct yourself, is not as straightforward as it might seem.

Summary of key points

If you are looking to collect straightforward information in a standardised way quickly and cheaply and without having to interact too closely with anyone then consider using a questionnaire.

Ensure that using a questionnaire really is the best method of data collection available to you in order to address your research question or the problem you wish to solve. Semi-structured questionnaires and individual research projects work particularly well together.

Always try to design your questionnaires to be simple, clear and brief. Consider question form, response mode and overall presentation carefully. Aim to make your questionnaire more inviting and less tedious to complete.

Avoid doing the things to be avoided! Ask only one question at a time and keep on task. Don't include anything that is not required. It will only lengthen the questionnaire distracting you and your respondents.

Using questionnaires with different audiences requires careful consideration. What is appropriate for a teacher is not always appropriate for a parent and what is appropriate for a 11-year-old is not always appropriate for a 5-year-old.

Further reading

The classic works on designing, constructing and using questionnaires are by Moser and Kalton (1977) and Oppenheim (1992). Oppenheim (1992), in particular, is a source you should definitely try to get a hold of and read if you can. The other texts presented here provide broadly similar advice and are well worth consulting.

Moser, C.A. and Kalton, G. (1977) *Survey methods in social investigations*. London: Heinemann.

Oppenheim, A.N. (1992) *Questionnaire design, interviewing and attitude measurement*. London: Pinter.

Simmons, R. (2008) Questionnaires. In: N. Gilbert (ed) *Researching social life*. London: Sage. 182–205.

Verma, G.K. and Mallick, K. (1999) *Researching education: perspectives and techniques*. London: Falmer.

6 Conversations with a purpose: research interviews

Learning outcomes

The research interview provides a means of collecting all sorts of data from all sorts of different people about all sorts of different things but in considerably more detail than a questionnaire. But interviewing can also be time consuming and subject to many different interviewer effects. By having read this chapter and completed the tasks within it, you will:

- know about the interview as a research tool and as a method for collecting data;

- be able to design and construct your own interview schedule in accordance with conventional practice;

- be able to conduct research interviews with confidence;

- be aware of some of the strengths and limitations of interviewing in educational research.

The interview as a research tool

The interview has been used throughout educational research for some time and defined in its most basic sense as everything from a process of communication and a means of collecting talk to a conversation with a purpose. But while terms such as *communication*, *talk* and *conversation* make the interview sound appealing and simple to do, nothing could be further from the truth. You will undoubtedly have been interviewed at one time or another yourself and know that interviews take place in different ways for different purposes. You will almost certainly have been interviewed before starting your own course and you may even have been interviewed already for your first teaching post or other work in education. We are concerned here with the research interview as the principal means of collecting data or for providing supplementary information for the purposes of clarification or triangulation. Interviewing is commonly employed in individual research projects if the aim is:

- to collect detailed information from a relatively small number of participants;

- to explore the nature of expressed views, opinions, perceptions, attitudes, preferences and behaviours by allowing specific lines of enquiry or matters of interest to be pursued as they arise and in depth;

- to achieve a relatively high level of personal interaction while maintaining an acceptable level of standardisation.

The interview, then, is a flexible research tool ideally suited to collecting data about what people know as well as about their relationships, experiences and feelings.

Designing, constructing and using interview schedules

Once settled upon the research interview as the best method of getting the data you need in order to answer your research question or to solve your problem you can then begin to think about designing an interview schedule. Research interviews usually take place between two people, an interviewer and an interviewee. At times, however, it may be beneficial to conduct paired or group interviews. Which you choose depends entirely on what your own project entails and the resources you have at your disposal. Focus group interviews represent a variation of the simple group interview. During a focus group interview, participants could, for example, be given some relevant matter of educational importance to discuss while you direct your attention to watching how the group interacts as well as to what the group has to say. Your only involvement might be to maintain the momentum of the discussion and to encourage participation. Whether interviewing on a one-to-one, paired or group basis, there may well be an *off the shelf* interview schedule available to you, of course, particularly if you are setting out to replicate something already appearing in the research literature. But as with questionnaires, time moves on, ideas change and the circumstances under which the interviews were conducted in any existing studies will never be exactly the same. Similarly, interview schedules are unlikely to appear published in full. They may, however, be pieced together from the descriptions of method and any transcripts appearing in the original texts. Considering only one-to-one interviews further, there are three basic types of research interview, the schedules for which vary accordingly.

- Structured or respondent-type – where the interviewer retains control of the agenda by asking mostly closed questions throughout (these are easier to analyse and normally undertaken for diagnostic purposes).

- Unstructured or informant-type – where the interviewee retains control of the agenda by responding to mostly open questions throughout (these are harder to analyse and normally undertaken for therapeutic purposes).

- Semi-structured – where control of the interview is shared or leans more one way or the other by using a mixture of questions (these are well suited to individual research projects).

While all work well in educational research provided you don't bite off more than you can chew in terms of sample size, semi-structured interviews probably offer most scope. In addition to questions, the research interview in education can also include any number of additional practical as well as intellectual tasks. While there may appear to be some overlap between the structured interview and the face-to-face and telephone questionnaire, the greater level of personal interaction involved in interviewing keeps them sufficiently distinct.

It's important when designing and constructing an interview schedule to remember that in order to be successful all interviewees must be able to fully understand what is being asked of them by you and you must be able to fully understand what the interviewees provide by way of response. As such, the language and presentation of questions and tasks must match the general ability level of interviewees be they children, teachers, parents or members of the general public. Questions should be sequenced such that they lead interviewees through the process of interview fluently and with ease and the sequence of questions or tasks should be planned to make the total interview experience continuous and purposeful. As such, it can be useful to ask the more challenging or difficult questions towards the middle or the end rather than at the start. Steps in the process of designing, constructing and using an interview schedule might be summarised as follows.

- Be clear about the nature and purpose of the data you need in relation to your research question or problem.

- Consider how many questions and tasks are necessary and the form and logical sequence these might take in order to probe effectively.

- Create a trial interview schedule and pilot and amend this accordingly paying particular attention to areas of concern raised in feedback.

- Conduct the interviews.

- Subject your data to an appropriate means of interrogation and analysis (usually leaning towards qualitative – though the quantitative analysis of interview data is perfectly acceptable).

It almost goes without saying that interviewing on a one-to-one basis in any situation requires a great deal of interpersonal awareness and skill and you should try to get as much interview practise and experience as possible before your actual research project gets underway. Piloting the interview schedule will help. You can demonstrate your awareness and skill straight away by making sure that you arrive to conduct your interviews on time and that any special equipment you need to use works. Turning up late when working in any professional capacity only to find that you have flat batteries for the audio-visual recording equipment or that you've left the power cable behind reflects badly not only on you but on your supervisor and course too. Make sure you negotiate where the interviewing is to take place (e.g. somewhere quiet, secure and non-threatening particularly if working with children) and give careful thought to the form of seating arrangement you need (e.g. shoulder to shoulder or across a table). You will only have a short time in which to establish a rapport with your interviewees so introduce yourself and remind each and every one what the interview is about. Be aware of interview stress at all times and be prepared to take a break or to stop an interview if it all starts to go horribly wrong. Stress can also be caused by working in an unsuitable location too. Good interviewers maintain eye contact, listen carefully and remain attentive at all times. Listening carefully and remaining attentive will help you to know when to probe more deeply and when to allow interviewees to elaborate, explore and explain more fully. It also lets interviewees know that you are genuinely interested in what they have to tell you. Non-verbal cues can give a lot away too so try to adopt an even and neutral tone of voice and be aware of your own body language. Towards the end of each interview, any unresolved matters should be clarified and confirmed and the interviewee thanked.

The responses provided during an interview may be recorded in writing or using any form of audio-visual means available to you. Note taking during an interview can be economical in terms of saving time later but unless you can write down everything said and done quickly and accurately you may miss out and lose a great deal of valuable information. It's also hard to note down things like tone of voice, inflection, changes in speed, exclamations, pauses, sighs, and so on. Leaving space for notes on the interview schedule itself can be helpful and you may need to develop your own form of shorthand or system for coding different sorts of response to speed things up. Audio-visual recording might be considered essential if all verbal and non-verbal information is to be gathered as fully and as objectively as possible while permitting time to devote to the interviewees where necessary. All such recordings take time to listen to, watch and transcribe. Some interviewees may find audio-visual recording both intrusive and inhibiting and may request that you not proceed in this way. With group or focus group interviews, some form of audio-visual recording will almost certainly be required. It's from your notes and other forms of recording that the transcripts, extracts, quotes and other data for your final report are obtained. It is not a good idea to try to remember what was said during an interview afterwards.

Worked example

Children's ideas

The task

Concept interviews which explore children's ideas about particular things across all curriculum areas are a common theme in individual research projects. Warwick was a final year BEd student specialising in English but looking to explore children's ideas in science and about the Earth in space in particular. Warwick's literature review had led him to several important articles, the authors of which had each adopted very different approaches but generally found the same thing. Many children think that the Earth is flat and not spherical in shape because that is how they *see* it every day and because it's flat you could easily fall off the edge. Knowing about children's ideas like this can fundamentally influence how you plan to teach. While most articles considered the Earth's shape and gravitational attraction, Warwick also wanted to elicit information about what the Earth looks like, how big it is, and so on. Being able to probe deeply in order to understand exactly what children mean is essential. Warwick knew that on his next placement he'd be in a position to interview up to 28 Year 6 children and that the *fieldwork* for the research had to be completed in one week. After some considerable working, reworking and further amendment, including some trialling in order to establish the best sequence of questions and language to use, his interview schedule started to take shape. Warwick decided to adopt a semi-structured approach by asking a combination of 12 open and closed questions and providing the interviewees with some simple tasks to complete too. The questions and tasks appearing on his interview schedule are presented as follows.

The Earth in space

1. What shape is the Earth?

2. Is there a shape here that's most like the Earth (selection provided)?

3. How do people know it's that shape?

4. Can you draw a picture of what you think the Earth would look like from space?

5. What colour would it be?

6. What would you expect to see all around it?

7. How come we can't see the Earth's *roundness* when we look out of the window?

8. How big is the Earth?

9. Have you ever heard of anybody falling off the Earth?

10. Could anybody ever fall off the Earth?

11. Can you find the Earth in this collection of pictures?

12. What is the Earth?

Sometimes even the simplest things need careful thought. You might wonder, for example, why so many questions directed towards the Earth's shape appear at the start of the interview and sort of work their way in throughout. Well, if you ask a class of children *What shape is the Earth?* many are likely to say *round*. You don't know from this if they mean round like a disk or round like a ball. Even if they mean round like a ball you don't know if they are simply repeating what they've been told or indicating what they truly believe. So ask the children to pick a shape from a selection of different shapes provided, one of which is a sphere, and justify their choice. Later, look at how they draw and describe the Earth. This is what is meant by methodological triangulation. In this case, methodological triangulation would allow Warwick to be more certain that the responses obtained during interview were internally consistent and therefore more valid. Hopefully you can deconstruct his interview schedule to appreciate the logic involved. Would you change anything to make it better? Warwick went on to arrange the interviews to take place in a quiet area of the school but near to the children's classroom. He had secretly hoped to interview more children across different year groups to carry out a comparative study but quickly realised that this would never happen. He simply didn't have time.

Things to be avoided

Pitfalls commonly associated with interviewing are presented as follows.

* Avoid dressing in a way which looks out of place or might indicate that you are an authority figure. This may require careful negotiation if working in an environment with a particular dress code. How you appear to your interviewees is important. If interviewing children in a school, for example, try not to look like

a teacher! The children will only respond to you like a teacher which may not be what you want.

- Avoid assuming a teaching role. Research interviews concern themselves with eliciting information not testing or interrogating. Resist correcting, altering or changing what is said and done. Try not to respond favourably or unfavourably even if told something which is wrong. After all, errors and misconceptions might be just what you're interested in.

- Avoid asking leading questions. These just introduce unwanted interviewer bias.

- Avoid making assumptions about what interviewees are thinking and don't interrupt or finish off what they have to say. Don't move on in an interview if you don't fully understand what has taken place. Anything else is just a bit rude.

- Avoid ending abruptly. Maybe go over what's been said and done to clarify and confirm. Then thank your interviewees for their time and trouble.

Reflective task

Getting the most out of your interviews

It's probably fair to say that interviewing individuals on a one-to-one basis is more common than interviewing pairs or groups. Group interviews are just that little bit more difficult to organise and manage. Making sure that all individuals in group situations participate is not as easy as it sounds and poring over recorded outcomes can be particularly onerous. However, at least one recently developed technique might make the challenges attached to group interviewing a thing of the past. Obtain a copy of the following article (print or online):

- Hopkins, E.A. (2009) Classroom conditions to secure enjoyment and achievement: the pupils' voice – listening to the voice of every child matters. *Education 3–13*, 37 (in press).

This article addresses the significance of *voice* within the contexts of *Every Child Matters*, *Excellence and Enjoyment* and the *Primary National Strategy*. As determined by the author, *voice* refers to the process of listening to the views and opinions of children about teachers and teaching and then using those views and opinions to more fully understand effective pedagogy by developing strategies for more personalised teaching and learning and improving classroom conditions. What makes this article particularly interesting is the adoption of the *Ishikawa* or *fishbone tool* from the business world to support the group interview and the analysis of data. The *fishbone tool* is so called because it looks to all intents and purposes just like a fishbone with a central spine and as many ribs as is necessary to complete the exercise. In one example, the author describes how a group of Year 4 children first identified what made their lessons enjoyable (the central spine of the fishbone if you like). Six different ribs emerged which were then labelled with key headings including subjects, teachers, activities, other children, feeling good and learning. The children then proceeded in a more focused manner to discuss what made lessons enjoyable by annotating each rib with more detail. Though relatively new in the educational world, the adoption of this technique seems entirely appropriate given that what counted here was the collective *voice* of the children involved.

Individual or one-to-one interviews just wouldn't have been *fit-for-purpose*. From your own reading of the article, what might you consider the pros and cons of this technique to be in relation to other forms of interviewing? Can you think of any limitations to its adoption and use? Can you think of any other examples of topics particularly well suited to this approach?

Working with children

Interviewing children, particularly in schools, can be a real pleasure and in the majority of instances children themselves enjoy being interviewed. Just remember to be patient, to ask your questions clearly and be prepared to ask your questions in different ways if necessary. It's not impossible either that you may need to prompt children a little more than adults but the rewards more than make up for it. Above all else, allow children to set the pace and don't patronise. Of course, children may still fail to understand the questions you ask or the tasks you set or be able to verbalise, draw or illustrate by any other means a response with which they are satisfied. There may be nothing you can do about any of that, of course, but don't forget to remind children that it's perfectly acceptable to say *I'm not sure*. At least this may help stop them simply making things up to look good or to think they're being helpful. All interviews should take place in a secure environment where you and the children feel safe and where interruptions can be kept to a minimum. If interviewing in a school, you will need to be flexible to fit in around what goes on during the normal school day. Schools and teachers will usually try to accommodate you to a point but their requirements will always take priority over yours. Try to be seen around the school before you start to interview in order for the children to become familiar with your presence. With younger children, particularly infants, interviews should be kept as short as possible and take no longer than about 30 minutes. With older children, particularly juniors, you might be able to sustain interest and enthusiasm for up to 1 hour. This means that you may only be able to interview about five or six children in any one day or a class of 30 children over the course of a week. Don't be too ambitious in terms of sample size. Interviewing groups of children may provide greater coverage but children also behave very differently in groups and this may not be to your advantage. Always make sure that those in authority in a school or elsewhere know what you are doing and that you have obtained permission.

Practical task

The flexibility of interviewing

Interviewing is a particularly flexible method for collecting data. A common mistake made by many experienced as well as inexperienced researchers, however, is to try to include far too many questions and tasks resulting in interviews which just take too long to complete or which collect far too much data than can ever be analysed sensibly. By way of an example, exploring children's views about collaborative

Practical task continued

learning, including the group skills required for collaborative work, need only require as few as four simple questions. Your skill as an interviewer lies in knowing how to prompt and probe effectively as responses emerge.

- Do you think you achieve more when working in groups?

- Do you prefer to work in groups picked by your teacher or picked by you?

- Which skills do you think are important for groups to work well together?

- Do you think people can be taught how to work well in groups?

Now try preparing some interview schedules on topics of your own. A few examples of trickier but fascinating topics are provided for you to begin with:

- sex (or drugs) education in primary schools;

- sibling support or rivalry;

- forms of bullying and their effects;

- educational experiences and the outdoor centre (or museum or gallery);

- the public perception of teaching.

In each case, begin by considering who might be involved (e.g. children, teachers, parents, members of the general public) and how this might influence your choice of questions and tasks. Refine your own interview technique by piloting your schedules with others and reflecting on the feedback they provide.

Strengths and limitations

Interviewing presents opportunities to probe deeply and in detail by being able to work with individuals, pairs or groups in different ways. The richness of data provided by interviewing can be impressive. The production of written records together with audio-visual recordings of events certainly helps reduce major sources of potential interviewer bias by addressing the conscious and unconscious selection of material you note down or, indeed, forget to note down. The audio-visual recording of interviews, while not absolutely necessary in every situation, just gives the edge in terms of making sure you don't lose exactly what you've gone to great lengths to secure. Interviewing and the subsequent transcription of any audio-visual materials can, however, be extremely time consuming, even if the number of people you interview is small. Talk can also be difficult to analyse and interpret. In any interview, both the interviewer and interviewee influence each other to a greater or lesser extent. Known interviewer effects include personal identity (e.g. age, sex, ethnic origin, accent, socio-economic status and professional status), self-presentation (e.g. appearance) and personal involvement (e.g. attentiveness and style). Interviewees may also differ in motivation to co-operate and to answer accurately and truthfully or may feel that you are not sufficiently interested in what they have to say or understand how they feel. In general, while the validity and reliability of interview responses are affected by all of these things, there are steps you can take to minimise the effects.

Summary of key points

If you are looking to collect detailed information from a relatively small number of participants by interacting with them in a fairly standardised way then consider the research interview.

Ensure that interviewing really is the best method of data collection available to you in order to address your research question or the problem you wish to solve. Semi-structured interviews and individual research projects work particularly well together.

Always try to design your interview schedule to be simple, clear and brief. Consider including tasks as well as asking questions and take care to match questions and tasks to the abilities of the interviewees.

Interviewing requires considerable interpersonal awareness and skill. Get as much practise and experience as you can.

Avoid doing the things to be avoided! Dress appropriately. Don't teach and don't be rude.

How you tackle interviewing adults might be very different to how you tackle interviewing children. Give careful thought to your audience.

Further reading

The classic works on designing and constructing interview schedules and interviewing are by Cannell and Kahn (1968) and Powney and Watts (1987). A clear and short review is also provided by Wragg (2002).

Cannell, C.F. and Kahn, R.L. (1968) Interviewing. In: G. Lindzay and E. Aronson (eds) *The handbook of social psychology (Vol.2)*. New York: Addison-Wesley. 526–595.

Fielding, N. and Thomas, H. (2008) Qualitative interviewing. In: N. Gilbert (ed) *Researching social life*. London: Sage. 245–265.

Keats, D. (2000) *Interviewing: a practical guide for students and professionals.* Maidenhead: Open University Press.

Powney, J. and Watts, M. (1987) *Interviewing in educational research.* London: Routledge.

Legard, R., Keegan, J. and Ward, K. (2003) In-depth interviews. In: J. Ritchie, and J. Lewis (eds) *Qualitative research practice: a guide for social science students and researchers.* London: Sage. 138–169.

Wragg, E.C. (2002) Interviewing. In: M. Coleman and A.R.J. Briggs (eds) *Research methods in educational leadership.* London: Paul Chapman. 143–158.

7. Seeing is believing: observation

Learning outcomes

Observation comes into its own as a research tool when looking to collect data as *eye-witness* accounts of what people say and do. When knowingly being observed, however, people don't always act as normally as they might do otherwise. By having read this chapter and completed the tasks within it, you will:

- know about observation as a research tool and as a method for collecting data;

- be able to design and construct your own observation schedule in accordance with conventional practice;

- be able to carry out formal observations with confidence;

- be aware of some of the strengths and limitations of observation in educational research.

Observation as a research tool

Observation is used in education if the purpose is to capture something of the dynamics and complexities of particular activities and events as they unfold right before your very eyes. You naturally observe what is going on around you every minute of every day, of course, but rarely would you ever do this as formally or as systematically as you would for an individual research project. You may already have been formally and systematically observed yourself, perhaps when teaching in a school on placement or in another location. If so, the rigour associated with observation will be very familiar to you. You'll also be very familiar with the stress of knowing that you're being observed and the effect this can have. The term *observation* can be quite misleading, however, for observation involves hearing as much as it does seeing. Indeed, observation may involve all of the senses depending on what it is you set out to observe and where the observation takes place. Observation is commonly employed in individual research projects if the aim is:

- to collect detailed information about what people actually do *in situ* by watching them and listening to them rather than by asking them;

- to explore people's actions, interactions and other behaviours in intimate detail while maintaining an acceptable level of standardisation.

Observation, then, either as the principal means of collecting data or for providing supplementary information for the purposes of clarification or triangulation, is an ideal research tool for investigating classroom-based practices and organisational cultures in all of their many and varied forms.

Designing, constructing and using observation schedules

When designing and constructing any observation schedule you first need to think carefully about exactly what it is you want to observe (e.g. actions, interactions or other behaviours), where the observation will take place (e.g. in a school, an outdoor centre, a museum or a gallery) and who will be involved (e.g. children, teachers, parents or members of the general public). As with questionnaires and interviews, there may well be an *off the shelf* observation schedule available to you, of course, particularly if you are setting out to replicate something already appearing in the research literature. But the same limitations apply in the sense that time moves on, ideas change and the circumstances under which any observations were conducted in any existing studies will never be exactly the same. Similarly, observation schedules are unlikely to appear published in full and may need to be pieced together from the descriptions of method and any findings appearing in the original texts. There are three basic types of observation, the schedules for which vary accordingly.

- Structured – where the observer sets out with a clearly determined agenda for what will be observed (these are easier to organise, manage, record and analyse).

- Unstructured – where the observer sets out with no pre-determined agenda for what will be observed (these are harder to organise, manage, record and analyse).

- Semi-structured – where the observer sets out with an agenda for what will be observed firmly in mind but this is sufficiently adaptable to accommodate unforeseen happenings (these are well suited to individual research projects).

Structured observations often prove too inflexible to cope with the dynamics and complexities of everyday situations. Unstructured observations often prove to be too loose and insufficiently focused to capture the importance of certain situations as they arise and happen all around you. They can also result in *sensory overload* and bewilderment. Semi-structured observations are probably most suited to most circumstances. The design and construction of an observation schedule will also be influenced by your own role in the observation process and the extent to which you feel it necessary to get involved. There are two ways to proceed:

- join in with those you are observing – referred to as participant observation;

- remain detached from those you are observing – referred to as non-participant observation.

Joining in with those you are observing and immersing yourself in the activities and events taking place presents clear opportunities to gain additional research insights by actually experiencing what is happening for yourself. Remaining detached from those you are observing is probably more common and, in many ways, certainly less demanding. Whether you choose to participate or not, and when studying education or training to be a teacher for the first time, you should openly discuss what you intend to do and why with those involved from the outset. Such disclosure is strongly advised. This may also lead to a negotiated and more productive observation agenda benefiting all. Undisclosed observation, which occurs when the purpose of your being present remains concealed from those you are observing, is ethically sensitive and potentially hazardous to say the least (e.g. consider all possible consequences of observing parents collecting children from school – an act which if spotted might easily be misconstrued as something more sinister). Some might see it as an act of betrayal!

Specific techniques for recording actions, interactions and other behaviours during an observation include:

- note taking (e.g. literally noting what is going on right there in front of you);

- frequency or tally counting (e.g. recording how often specific actions, interactions or behaviours occur using a simple tick chart);

- interval sampling (e.g. recording on a chart what is going at specific time intervals of say every 1 minute or so);

- duration sampling (e.g. noting on a chart how long particular actions, interactions or behaviours last);

- activity or event rating (e.g. measuring or scoring the effect of particular actions, interactions or behaviours using a numerical scale);

- taking photographs (e.g. capturing still images of actions, interactions and behaviours as they happen);

- audio-visual recording (e.g. capturing whole observations for later analysis).

Taking notes is relatively easy to do and provides an ongoing record of activities and events as well as allowing you to record critical incidents, interruptions and unforeseen happenings without too much difficulty. Trying to write down absolutely everything said and done quickly and accurately while observing at the same time, however, is no easy task. As with interviewing, taking notes is not so good for recording what is *said* and *done* non-verbally either. Using charts and numerical scales is certainly useful if you know what you are looking out for in advance (this is why piloting your observation schedule is important), but charts and scales have a tendency to get longer and longer and more and more cumbersome to use. Photographs only record an instant in time, of course, and need to be accompanied by written descriptions to preserve context and meaning. Audio-visual recording offers the greatest flexibility in terms of capturing everything that you might want to observe as fully, as accurately and as objectively as possible and for later interrogation and analysis when you have more time. This assumes that those being observed don't mind and that any potential problems with obtaining and locating the audio-visual equipment can be overcome. Sociograms which allow you to record in diagrammatic form who talks to whom about what and for how long during group work or in a meeting can also be useful. Which techniques are available to you, to be used individually or in combination, will depend very much on the form your observations take (e.g. structured, unstructured or semi-structured, participant or non-participant, disclosed or undisclosed). Steps in the process of designing, constructing and using an observation schedule might be summarised as follows.

- Be clear about the nature and purpose of the data you need in relation to your research question or problem.

- Consider what you want to observe, your role in the observation process (participant or non-participant) and how many observations might be required.

- Create a trial observation schedule and pilot and amend this accordingly paying particular attention to areas of concern raised in feedback.

- Conduct the observations having usually disclosed everything in advance.

- Subject your data to an appropriate means of interrogation and analysis (leaning towards qualitative or quantitative as directed by the recording techniques employed).

When looking to do any form of observational research, always remember that the focus of your work might turn out to be an *all or nothing deal* with no chance of a repeat performance (e.g. a particular meeting or a particular assembly at school). Preparation is everything. It might equally revolve around something like a sequence of lessons in a particular curriculum area in which case missing out on just one may not be so much of an issue. Don't forget to record details of the physical environment in which any observation takes place (e.g. in the form of an annotated room plan) and don't forget to ask for a copy of any relevant documentation (e.g. a lesson plan). The logistics involved in setting up even one observation never mind more can present some very real challenges. Be mindful of this at the planning stage of your project.

Worked example

Observing teachers and young children

The task

Observing lessons in schools is a productive way of investigating the dynamics and complexities of teaching and learning during normal classroom-based activities, particularly if it's the actions, interactions and other behaviours of those involved that lie at the heart of your research. Dee was on a three-year BA degree course in primary education leading to Qualified Teacher Status. Dee had decided to make full use of a special week-long research trip to an infant school to collect the data she needed for her individual research project. Dee knew she'd be in a Year 1 class and was interested in the basic structure of lessons, the role her class teacher adopted and the strategies she used when teaching, and how the children responded to the activities presented. Dee considered the work to fall into three natural stages.

- Pre-observation planning.

- Observation (over several lessons).

- Post-observation follow-up.

1. Pre-observation planning

Dee quickly established that she would need to carry out a small number of disclosed, non-participant observations running over several lessons requiring more than one semi-structured observation schedule to avoid her work from becoming too superficial. On arriving at the school, and in consultation with her class teacher, Dee agreed which lessons would be observed and how she and the class teacher would try to minimise any distractions by having her present in the room but not teaching herself. The class teacher was interested in knowing more about Dee's research findings and was fully supportive, providing Dee with copies of all relevant lesson plans. Dee prepared a comprehensive drawing of the layout of the classroom showing table and seating arrangements and where she would sit herself. She also calculated the ages of the children in months from dates of birth in the attendance register and gathered together as much useful background information about the children as she could.

2. Observation

Dee's initial reading of the research literature and trawling of the internet was useful to a point but there were no observation schedules available that she felt really fitted the bill and that she could use directly. After some careful thought, however, she finally prepared the two observation schedules presented.

Her schedule for observing whole lessons has several features worth pointing out. Not only does it offer the potential to record the structure of any lesson observed in terms of the duration of individual lesson phases, it provides a means by which specific teacher strategies can be logged as each lesson proceeds. This provides the opportunity to monitor not only the frequency or occurrence of particular actions, interactions and behaviours but to note where they occur in the body of a lesson itself (only 10 minutes of which are shown for simplicity). Additional information, including non-verbal communication, can also be logged in the notes column. Dee also inserted a scale for recording the self-perceived level of classroom noise. In this instance, from *silence* (1) to *unbearable* (5). Dee's own drawing of the layout of the classroom also provided her with a way of recording where the class teacher positioned herself in the room in the same one minute intervals.

When considering her schedule for observing children at work, Dee tried to be a little more ambitious. Focusing on the on-task/off-task behaviour of children sitting in groups of up to six, she also hoped to be able to use a form of sociometric analysis involving the construction of sociograms (which in their most basic sense use single arrowed or double arrowed lines drawn between individuals to indicate who talks to whom during a discussion and in which direction the discussion takes place). This she would do by dividing the observation up into two separate parts (only ten minutes of each are shown for simplicity). Dee was aware that sociograms can be relatively easy to construct when working with older children or adults but was determined to find out if they could be used productively with younger children too. Dee's schedule for observing groups, particularly Part 1, was simple and straightforward in every aspect of its construction. Not only would it be possible to see which children were on and off-task as the group work took place, but the nature of what was being said and done could be recorded in the notes. The table and seating arrangement for the construction of a sociogram in Part 2 provided a useful template for getting underway quickly and efficiently.

Whole class lesson observation

Date: Time:
Lesson: Class size:
Teacher: Other adults:

Lesson structure	Duration (minutes)
Introduction
Group work
Plenary/discussion	

Teaching	Time (minutes)										Notes
	1	2	3	4	5	6	7	8	9	10	
Introduces											
Describes											
Explains											
Models											
Reminds											
Asks questions											
Gives answers											
Corrects											
Directs											
Behaviour											
Gives praise											
Encourages											
Reprimands											
Negotiates											
Noise											
Level (1 to 5)											

Group observation

Part 1:

Date: Time:
Lesson: Group size:
Teacher: Other adults:

Behaviour	Time (minutes)										Notes
	1	2	3	4	5	6	7	8	9	10	
On-task/off-task											
1.											
2.											
3.											
4.											
5.											
6.											

Part 2:

Table and seating arrangement:

Notes (at one minute intervals):

1.
2.
3.
4.
5.
6.
7.
8.
9.
10.

3. Post-observation

Dee was aware of the importance of post-observation feedback and made every effort to interview those involved obtaining.

- notes from discussion with teacher afterwards (perception of teaching and learning);

- notes from discussion with children afterwards (perception of teaching and learning).

Dee really gave herself a lot to do but in the end the effort was worth it. She managed to observe several lessons, mostly literacy, and shared her findings with the class teacher who was able to reflect on the outcomes and improve certain aspects of her own planning and delivery. Disappointingly, Dee found the construction of sociograms just too demanding for the simple reason that there was too much going on at any one time. Looking at Dee's schedules, would you change anything to make them better?

Things to be avoided

Pitfalls commonly associated with observation are presented as follows.

- Avoid looking out of place. If observing children in a school, for example, you need to find a way of becoming *invisible* in order to minimise distraction.

- Avoid being tempted to intervene, to help out or to teach. This applies when observing in any teaching and learning environment. Unless intentionally participating, don't get involved unless there is a very good reason to do so.

- Avoid being intrusive in proceedings. Whether participating in what you are observing or not, don't interrupt the natural flow of things.

- Avoid making assumptions about what those being observed are thinking or doing. Don't leave without discussing to clarify intentions and meanings, otherwise your interpretation of events might be completely wrong.

- Avoid being judgemental. It's easy to watch people at work doing what they do and think that you could do it better. It's just as easy to let this slip into your final report. Best not.

(Reflective task)

Seeing it for yourself

Observation is often considered to be one of the more effective tools for collecting data because observers get to see and hear for themselves what is going on right there in front of them. In education in particular, observation often appears to take pride of place when it comes to studying teaching and learning in the classroom-based environments of schools and other locations. But should observation really command such respect? Obtain a copy of the following article (print or online):

- Byard, K. (2002) Is seeing really believing? Observation lessons from a teacher's perspective. *Education 3–13*, 30(2): 56–61.

Here, the author describes his own experiences of teaching a Year 6 numeracy class of 30 top-ability children in a junior school while being observed by the head. Read the article carefully paying particular attention to the sections on behaviour (the author's as teacher as well as the children's) and the effect of simply having an observer in the room. This article presents a particular observation scenario, of course, in that the observation is formal and being carried out by a more senior colleague acting in a strictly professional capacity. If you've ever been formally observed teaching in a school yourself, much of what the author writes might seem familiar. But there are broader lessons to be learnt here too. Use this author's experiences to consider carefully the potential impact of you observing teachers and children at work and what you could do to minimise such observer effects. Which other ways of operating or collecting data might you choose to adopt in order to ensure the validity and reliability of findings? Is seeing really believing after all?

Working with children

Having the time to really observe children at work and play, particularly in a school, is a luxury, so make the most of it if the opportunity arises. Children are naturally curious about having any stranger come in to their classroom, of course, and they'll always want to know what you're doing. The trouble is, they always want to know what you're doing when you're trying to observe them acting naturally. If you can, get into school as often as possible in advance so that the children get familiar with having you around. Sometimes, children will approach you for help when you're hard at work yourself. Perhaps explain to them in advance what you are doing, that you really need to concentrate hard and that you won't be able to help on this occasion but will do later. Just make sure you do! Knowing they're being observed, many children will *play up* or behave out of character. There's really nothing you can do about this except to note that this is what you think is going on and to account for it afterwards. Being observed can be stressful no matter how much effort you go to make those involved feel relaxed. If your observations happen to form part of an individual child study in particular, take great care to deal with this as sensitively as possible. Think how you would feel if singled out for such close attention. Always make sure that those in authority in a school or elsewhere know what you are doing and that you have obtained permission.

Practical task

Look and listen

Observation requires great skill and the ability to record actions, interactions and other behaviours quickly and accurately. On most occasions, most of what you observe will probably not involve any self-participation and those being observed will know exactly what you're doing and why. That said, it really all depends on the nature of your topic, your research question or problem, and what you hope to achieve. The recording technique or selection of techniques you choose should also carefully match the task or tasks ahead of you for these will ultimately determine the quality of data gathered and whether your analysis leans towards the quantitative or qualitative. Give some thought to the planning required to observe any or all of the following school-based examples.

- Teachers in different types of meeting or gathering (e.g. formally or informally at staff meetings, year group meetings or in the staffroom during breaks).

- Teachers interacting with parents (e.g. formally and informally before and after the start of the school day or at parents' evenings).

- Teachers interacting with children across different age groups (e.g. formally and informally during lessons or during other times of the school day).

- Children interacting with other children (e.g. formally and informally during lessons, around the school or in the playground).

Would your planning be affected in any way if your individual research project was based elsewhere (e.g. in an outdoor centre, a museum or a gallery)? Now try preparing an observation schedule to meet the demands associated with any one of these plans. Alternatively carry out the same exercise on a proposed observation of your own choice. Pilot the schedule with others on your own course and consider the feedback they provide.

Strengths and limitations

Perhaps the single greatest strength found in observing activities and events lies in the provision of first-hand, *eye-witness* accounts of what people say and do without actually having to ask them. Nevertheless, seeking confirmation of intentions and meanings is essential in order to ensure the validity and reliability of any subsequent interpretation. Some activities and events can also unfold at considerable pace and careless observation can result in the over-simplification and trivialisation of particularly dynamic and sometimes complex situations. While repeated observations using varied recording techniques may help, the opportunity to observe things more than once is not always available. Observing people at work or at play, be they children, teachers, parents or members of the general public, can become quite a personal and intimate matter and all observations need to be handled with care. Observation can also become quite value-laden (e.g. by having decided that there's something you want to observe in the first place) and selective on the part of the observer too (e.g. by observing only what you want to and not what you should) and such observer effects should be minimised at all costs. Always be mindful of the fact that people change simply by being observed.

Summary of key points

If you are looking to collect detailed information about people's actions, interactions and behaviours in situ then consider observation.

Ensure that observation really is the best method of data collection available to you in order to address your research question or the problem you wish to solve. Non-participant, semi-structured observations and individual research projects work particularly well together. Always declare your intentions.

Observation can be both demanding and tiring. It certainly requires concentration. Get as much practise and experience as you can.

Always try to design your observation schedule to be simple, clear and brief. Include a small selection of different techniques if time and opportunity permit.

Avoid doing the things to be avoided! Don't get in the way even if participating.

How you tackle observing adults might be very different from how you tackle observing children. Give careful thought to your audience. If observing children, try to remain as invisible as possible and keep an eye open for changes in behaviour brought about by your own presence.

Further reading

The classic works on designing and constructing observation schedules and observing are by Croll (1987) and Wragg (1994). The other texts presented here provide broadly similar advice and are well worth consulting.

Cavendish, S., Galton, M., Hargreaves, L. and Harlen, W. (1990) *Observing activities*. London: Paul Chapman.

Croll, P. (1987) *Systematic classroom observation*. London: Falmer.

Lofland, J. and Lofland, L. (eds) (2004) *Analysing social situations: a guide to qualitative observation*. London: Wadsworth.

Moyles, J. (2002) Observation as a research tool. In: M. Coleman and R.J. Briggs (eds) *Research methods in educational leadership and management*. London: Paul Chapman. 172–195.

Wragg, E.C. (1994) *An introduction to classroom observation*. London: Routledge.

8. From the past to the here and now: documents and documentary research

Learning outcomes

Documents provide a rich source of data on all sorts of different things which can be used for all sorts of different purposes. Documentary research comes into its own, however, when attempting to make sense of past events and present day situations. But not everything that finds its way into print can be trusted. By having read this chapter and completed the tasks within it, you will:

- know about documentary research and using documents as a method for collecting data;

- be able to undertake documentary research with confidence and in accordance with conventional practice;

- be aware of some of the strengths and limitations of using documents in educational research.

The document as a research tool

Documentary research in education is often difficult to pin down for it represents both an approach as well as a method for collecting data. Wherever you feel the emphasis lies, documents offer considerable research potential. You may already have some experience of documentary research without even knowing it. Long before you ever applied for the course you're enrolled on now, for example, you may have read and evaluated the prospectuses published by different institutions and browsed their websites looking for further information. If you did, you were using documents for research, albeit research of a personal nature. Similarly, if you've already worked in schools or in other locations, perhaps on placement, you may have had to read and evaluate the contents of policy documents, children's workbooks or guides for the general public. If you did, you were using documents for research. Documentary research is commonly employed in individual research projects if the aim is:

- to consider historical developments and changes in education using the information about people, places and events already available in the public domain;

- to explore developments and changes of a more recent or current nature using the information provided in documents which make their appearance during a period of active research or which are created specifically at the request of a researcher.

Documentary research, then, is ideally suited to work both in the library and the classroom and when investigating matters of an educational nature ranging in scope from policy to practice. It's important, however, not to confuse documentary research with the literature review. It's easy to get the two confused. When carrying out a literature review, you are involved in selecting and using information from various documents including academic journals and textbooks in order to contextualise your own work for your own benefit and for the benefit of the reader. When carrying out documentary research, documents such as academic journals and textbooks become the actual focus of investigation and sources of data themselves.

What kinds of document exist?

Leaving aside academic journals and textbooks, the range of educational documents available to you is vast and includes:

- Ofsted inspection reports and published performance data (e.g. for schools, colleges, universities and prisons);

- consultation reports;

- policy documents, curriculum documents, planning documents and schemes of work;

- examination papers and tests;

- newsletters, memos and minutes of meetings (e.g. board of governors, staff, parent-teacher);

- attendance registers;

- children's textbooks and workbooks;

- autobiographical and biographical accounts, personal diaries and logs;

- magazines and newspapers (e.g. *The Times Educational* and *Higher Education Supplements*);

- prospectuses, pamphlets and leaflets;

- educational websites obtained via the internet (e.g. the websites of schools, colleges, universities, outdoor centres, museums and galleries).

Beyond its traditional base in the written or printed word, documentary research also embraces the *text* arising from visual images, artefacts and sounds and alternative *documents* including artworks, photographs, films, advertising, television and radio broadcasts and pieces of music.

Using documents in research

All educational documents are products of their time and firmly embedded within whichever educational and cultural contexts prevailed when they were produced. Documents are also usually written or prepared for a particular audience in response to a particular set of circumstances. You may find that the contents of some documents relate directly to your individual research project while others contain only incidental information which may be of some use nevertheless. When poring over any document, it's important to be aware of what is obviously being reported or stated as well as to be aware of what requires more interpretation and reading between the lines. As indicated through its aims, documentary research is complicated by the fact that not all of the documents you might need for your individual research project actually exist at the time it begins. Just sometimes, useful documents get published when your research is well underway but not too late (e.g. a policy document, an Ofsted report, a series of lesson plans). At other times, you may need to have certain documents created for you. Data collection using personal diaries is increasingly popular in educational research, for example, and these, like questionnaires and interview and observation schedules, may be structured, unstructured or semi-structured in form. As with all other methods of data collection, how you choose to have information recorded in a personal diary, as well as what you choose to do with it afterwards, is very important. The steps and procedures associated with documentary research are very straightforward.

- Be clear about the nature and purpose of your work, the role of the documents and the data you need in relation to your research question or problem.

- Establish quickly where the documents you need most urgently are located or have to be produced and whether or not special permission is required to obtain them.

- Gather all relevant documents together, copying those you consider most important or need access to regularly if necessary (observing all copyright restrictions).

- Carry out the research adopting a strictly professional and ethical approach at all times but especially if your research topic or the information contained in any documents is sensitive or intrusive.

- Subject your data to an appropriate means of interrogation and analysis (leaning towards quantitative or qualitative depending on the type of information available to you and what you plan to do with it).

Worked example

Personal diaries

The task

Sally was in the final year of a Foundation Degree course in education. Being a bit sporty herself, she was particularly interested in children's health and fitness and keen to know if there was any difference in the weekly exercise routines of boys and girls. On her final placement, Sally would be placed in a primary school and have the opportunity to work with 7, 9 and 11-year-olds. As part her individual research project, Sally intended to have the children in the school keep a personal exercise diary which she designed as shown. The *How did you feel?* column was an attempt to gauge physical exertion and the children would be required to insert a number on a 5-point scale ranging from 1=I felt no noticeable difference to 5=I felt really out of breath and hot. The diaries would be supported with a questionnaire designed to explore the children's interest in exercise, their motivation for doing it and what barriers they faced if any. The sensitive nature of her work meant that she had to approach parents and obtain their permission in advance. The parents of the 7 and 9-year-olds were also asked for their support in helping the children to keep their diaries up-to-date. Sally also went to great lengths to avoid any embarrassment associated with individual health issues and cultural factors.

My exercise diary

Name: **Date:**

	What did you do?	Where did you do it?	Who did you do it with?	How long did it last?	How did you feel?
Before school					
Morning break					
Lunchtime					
Afternoon break					
PE lesson					
After school					

How did you get to school from home today?

Walked
Cycled
By car/bus

How far did you walk or cycle and how long did it take?

How did you get home from school today?

Walked
Cycled
By car/bus

How far did you walk or cycle and how long did it take?

Which form of exercise did you enjoy doing the most today and why?

As her placement and individual research project unfolded, the children's diaries were kept reasonably well and Sally was able to obtain copies of the school's PE policy, its scheme of work for PE and her class teacher's own lesson plans for PE spanning the duration of the investigation. Information from all of these additional documents and the questionnaire provided Sally with all that she needed to make a very real contribution to a particularly high profile subject.

Things to be avoided

In the same way that using the internet requires you to become an accomplished *Internet Detective*, don't assume that just because a document exists it's *safe* to use. Pitfalls commonly associated with using documents are presented as follows.

- Avoid using documents which do not appear authentic or genuine. When looking at any published documents either in print or online, take particular care to find out something about their provenance or where they came from. Do they appear *real* or *forged*? Professional documents in particular, including those passed around from one school to the next or from one teacher to another, often get modified or changed and end up bearing no resemblance to their originals. The more often this happens, the more likely it is for errors to appear and ambiguities to creep in. Try to find originals if you can.

- Avoid using documents which appear to lack credibility or trustworthiness. Documents can be produced by anybody and published anywhere. There are usually good reasons for writing and publishing, of course, but these aren't always made clear. What do you know about the authors and the publishers involved or about what drives their interest and motivation? Are you reading already recycled or second, third and fourth-hand accounts of other people's work? Does what you're reading appear biased or distorted?

- Avoid using documents that may not be representative. It's common in education to find different interpretations of the same event. Such interpretations often find their way into print within days of each other or at intervals spanning several decades. Are the expressed views and opinions reasonable and based on sound evidence? Now and again, you might come across an interpretation of an event which is at odds with everything else you've read. If the oddity is the only thing you've read then you're in trouble.

- Avoid introducing any unnecessary subjectivity when considering the *text* arising from visual images, artefacts and sounds. The principles of establishing authenticity, credibility and representativeness apply every bit as much to alternative *documents* as they do to the more conventional.

Reflective task

Creativity

Documentary research is well suited to library as well as classroom-based projects. The two are not mutually exclusive, of course, and sometimes it is possible to use documents to contribute towards current debate as much as it is possible to contribute towards current practice. Much documentary research often goes unnoticed quite possibly because it's more familiar with what gets read all the time rather than something with a unique character. Obtain a copy of the following article (print or online):

- Turner-Bisset, R. (2007) Performativity by stealth: a critique of recent initiatives on creativity. *Education 3–13*, 35(2): 193–203.

Creativity is difficult to define and as such has come to mean very different things to very different people. Within the context of primary education, creativity has taken on its very own meaning and, according to this author at least, has become enmeshed with the performance-driven culture which has now permeated throughout all schools. This article is of interest for two main reasons. Firstly, it illustrates how documents are used for research rather than a review of literature. This is an important distinction and one you need to be very much aware of. Secondly, it illustrates how documents can be unpicked or deconstructed to reveal one set of views and opinions underpinned by one set of values and beliefs and challenged with a different set of views and opinions underpinned by a different set of values and beliefs. From your own reading of this article, can you identify some of the main characteristics of documentary research? Does the author convince you using the evidence and interpretation presented that the discourse of creativity has been hijacked by central policy-makers and wrapped up in what she describes as *performativity*?

Working with children

Undertaking any documentary research which involves working with children requires careful consideration. Whether you set out to use existing documents or to have them created for you at your request, an ethical approach observing the privacy, anonymity and confidentiality of individuals is paramount. In schools, for example, you may find that you have relatively unrestricted access to various documents containing information of a highly personal nature. These might include attendance registers, development profiles, individual education plans, statements, report cards and test scores, not to mention workbooks. Only seek to collect and use those items which you need and to report their contents with due regard to the feelings of those concerned. Similarly, if looking to use children's workbooks to investigate such things as the effectiveness of teaching and learning, marking strategies or the quality of teacher feedback, just imagine for a moment how you would feel if somebody walked into your classroom and started doing this to you. Asking children to keep personal diaries certainly sounds appealing but you can't ask them to keep diaries on just anything. The more intrusive the information you require becomes, the more concerned teachers and parents will get. Personal diaries also usually require children to keep records of what they do in their own time outside of the normal school day. Some children may exaggerate what they write down. Others may forget to write down anything at all, and some who can't read or write so well may feel excluded. Don't expect personal diaries to be kept accurately for prolonged periods of time. On a cautionary note, take care if asked to amend or add new pages to a school's website not to include images of children which might place you at the centre of any child protection allegation. Always make sure that those in authority in a school or elsewhere know what you are doing and that you have obtained permission.

Practical task

Planning to use documents

Consider which documents you would need to set out and find in order to investigate each of the following topics.

- The introduction and subsequent evolution of the National Curriculum from 1989 to 1999 (or your own subject specialism within it).

- The portrayal of teaching as a profession (including the recent newspaper and television campaign promoted by the Training and Development Agency to attract applicants).

- Teaching, learning and children's academic progress at school (or within one curriculum subject at school).

- Truancy and its effect.

- The history of school inspection.

- Grade inflation from schools to universities.

- The nature and content of your own course (education or Initial Teacher Training) and its assessment framework.

Which of these topics would you consider to be more ethically sensitive or intrusive than others? Can you think of any topics of your own which would require the use of specific documents and which might qualify as documentary research?

Strengths and limitations

Most of the documents encountered during your individual research project are likely to be authoritative sources of information and factually accurate in what they present. Many important documents may also be found via online databases or using the internet, all of which may prove cost-effective both in time and in money. Never accept any single document at face value, however, and be particularly mindful to establish or reassure yourself of its authenticity, credibility and representativeness. Not to do so will simply destroy any attempt to establish validity and reliability. It's also important to try to minimise researcher bias in terms of what you extract and use from documents, particularly if this involves the views, opinions and interpretations of others. Documents such as personal diaries created during the period of your research and at your request are subject to the same design limitations as questionnaires and interview and observation schedules. Even if your research using personal diaries goes well, it may be difficult to establish the meaning behind entries. Perhaps the greatest limitation of using documents when studying education or training to be a teacher for the first time is that you can lose all personal contact with people themselves. Not in every situation, of course, but it can happen.

Summary of key points

Documentary research is really useful if you are looking to study something which happened in the past. If there's something you wish to study now, you can always have the documents you need created for you.

Ensure that using documents really is the best method of data collection available to you in order to address your research question or the problem you wish to solve.

Documents come in many different forms as does the text they present. Always consider the full breadth and scope of documents available to you and use them wisely.

Always take the time and effort to convince yourself that the documents you use are authentic, credible and representative. In other words, avoid doing the things to be avoided!

If using documents containing sensitive or personal information about particular individuals or particular situations, act ethically at all times.

Documentary research works well in the classroom as much as it does in the library. You can choose how much interaction to have with other people.

Further reading

The classic works on documentary research are by Platt (1981) and Scott (1990). The other texts presented here provide broadly similar advice and are well worth consulting.

MacDonald, K. (2008) Using documents. In: N. Gilbert (ed) *Researching social life*. London: SAGE. 285–303.

Morrison, M. (2002) Using diaries in research. In: M. Coleman and R.J. Briggs (eds) *Research methods in educational leadership and management*. London: Paul Chapman. 213–232.

Platt, J. (1981) Evidence and proof in documentary research. *The Sociological Review*, 21(1): 31–66.

Prior, L. (2003) *Using documents in social research*. London: Sage.

Scott, J. (1990) *A matter of record*. Cambridge: Polity Press.

9. Making sense of data: analysing numbers and words

Learning outcomes

Collecting data is one thing, making sense of it is something else entirely. Just what do you do with the numbers and words sitting in front of you? By having read this chapter and completed the tasks within it, you will:

- know about the most common means of analysing data and the differences between them;

- be able to organise and manage your own data confidently and effectively;

- be aware of when and how to present data using tables, charts and graphs.

What next?

Imagine the scenario. You never thought for one minute that you'd collect so much data, but there it all is. Whether in the form of completed and returned questionnaires, interview transcripts, observations or extracts from documents, you now have the opportunity to lift the lid on things for the first time and experience the most exciting part of the research process. There are no scripts or blueprints for how to go about analysing your data, of course, for things are never quite that simple. But you shouldn't have to ask yourself or your supervisor what to do next either. You should have given at least some thought to data analysis during the initial planning stage of your individual research project and not be worrying about it now. Either by design or by luck, however, you may be guided towards a particular form of data analysis depending upon:

- your own topic and the nature of your own research question or problem;

- any conventions attached to the approach or method of data collection you adopted;

- the type of data you collected itself;

- the procedures already used by others if replicating an existing study.

What is meant by data analysis?

Data analysis is often considered to be difficult but it's really only as difficult as you make it. Essentially, data analysis involves taking what you have apart, examining it in detail, and then putting it all back together again in a more condensed and meaningful way. Most individual research projects go through the same five basic stages of data analysis.

- Familiarisation.

- Reduction.

- Synthesis or collation.

- Description.

- Interpretation.

Familiarisation should take place even as the data come in. During this stage, you should be thinking carefully about what's going on, what everything is turning out to look like and what problems, if any, need to be resolved. Early familiarisation with your own data will certainly help when it comes to reducing it. Reduction concerns itself with sifting through the volume of *raw* data sitting in front of you and considering how best to organise it into smaller and more manageable chunks. As reduction takes place, your data should start to make more sense as perhaps patterns, trends, relationships and the like begin to emerge. Once things start to make more sense you should be able to synthesise or collate your data by bringing together what needs to be brought together in order to compare and contrast matters *internally* and *externally* alongside other works and to form a clearer picture of what is emerging. By now, your data will have given rise to what you might call findings and these need to be described by way of account and commentary and perhaps summarised in tables, charts and graphs or other forms of illustration. As you come to interpret your findings during the final stage of analysis, you should give relevance to your findings by providing explanations and drawing conclusions. While it doesn't have to be difficult, data analysis can certainly be messy. On occasion, for example, you might even start out doing something one way only to discover that doing it another way might be better. Changing direction mid-analysis can be time consuming and painful but nevertheless productive. It's all perfectly normal. In the initial stages of data reduction, particularly if faced with large amounts of data, it's easy to lose sight of essential detail. At the same time, it's also easy to fragment or *atomise* your data too much. Take great care not to ignore or to omit things just because they don't *fit* as well as great care not to make everything *fit* better when it doesn't or make it up. All outcomes are meaningful, even if you don't find what you expected.

Reflective task

Data analysis

In order to be able to analyse your data effectively, you have to be familiar with it, be able to reduce it to a more manageable size, identify how best to synthesise or collate it and then describe and interpret it. Obtain a copy of the following article (print or online):

- Silver, A. and Rushton, B.S. (2008) Primary-school children's attitudes towards science, engineering and technology and their images of scientists and engineers. *Education 3–13*, 36(1): 51–67.

This article considers how 120 Year 5 children, together with some of their parents and teachers, view science, engineering and technology. While the authors used a questionnaire developed from the work of others, its multi-faceted 5-section design allowed for the collection of both quantitative and qualitative data. Read the article carefully, but concentrate on the methodology, results and discussion. Can you identify the five basic stages of data analysis? Do the authors make it clear how they used their *raw* data to obtain and then manipulate the numbers and words they needed? The authors summarise their work using tables, bar charts and examples of children's drawings. Do you think they made the right choices? It's easy when reading articles to skip over findings presented in such ways but it's important that you don't. As chance would have it, the same authors supplemented their method of data collection with classroom-based discussions during an extension investigation. This work they refer to as *in press* with the same journal. When it eventually appears (in Volume 37), go through this task again comparing and contrasting outcomes.

Quantitative vs qualitative

It's all very well knowing what data analysis is and about the stages involved when doing it, but these things tell you nothing about the specific analytical techniques required. Most methods of data collection ultimately give rise to numbers and words and most individual research projects usually end up having to deal with both (though not necessarily in equal amounts). Quantitative data, namely data in the form of numbers, are usually treated statistically. Qualitative data, namely data in the form of words, are usually treated in terms of their content. Generally speaking, mention statistics and people's eyes glaze over. That's because they think of statistics as equations and tests which are difficult to understand. Descriptive statistics, which is all we are interested in here, however, only concerns itself with the likes of how many things are involved, how often certain things crop up or how long something takes. Most of the time, all you have to able to do is add up, subtract, multiply, divide and calculate percentages and averages (and if you can't do any of these things then you really are in trouble). Descriptive statistics also covers how to present data in tables, charts and graphs which help to summarise and visualise sometimes complex information. Those strongly opposed to working with numbers in education are often heard to trot out lines like *we work with people not numbers*, but such views are simply ill-informed. By not engaging with numbers in educational research you simply exclude yourself from most of the educational research literature available to you. While it is perfectly possible to *design* numbers or words out of a study, doing so is just not helpful. At the risk of being somewhat unforgiving, handling numbers, in one form or other, is as unavoidable as handling words. It's no more and no less difficult. So if you have a number hang up, get over it! You have to be fluent in handling both.

Practical task

Credibility, reality and ambiguity

There is a trend in education for people to consider themselves as quantitative researchers or qualitative researchers or at least to concentrate on only one form of research or the other. There's nothing wrong with this, of course, but the nature of education and the research that sometimes has to be done in order to understand the educational world doesn't always recognise such clear cut distinctions. When studying education or training to be a teacher for the first time, it might be better to consider what you do in terms of *fitness-for-purpose*. This means learning to accept that all forms of research and data are equally valuable.

- Can you think of any situations when you could justifiably only work with numbers or only work with words?

- Go to your library and flick through a random selection of articles from the education journals currently on display. Can you find any in which numbers or words have been completely *designed* or *filtered* out? Would you describe this as *the norm*?

- Consider the worked examples included within the method chapters presented earlier (questionnaires, interviews, observations and documents). What do you think the strengths and limitations of attempting to collect both quantitative and qualitative data might be?

- If you are about to start your own individual research project, whether it be attached to a placement in a school, an outdoor centre, a museum or a gallery or not, can you think where any quantitative and qualitative data might come from?

Even if your own course requires that you undertake a piece of quantitative or qualitative research, whatever that means, it's really hard to filter out numbers or words completely so don't try. Your research really will benefit as a consequence.

At a much deeper level, the terms *quantitative* and *qualitative* in education are highly loaded and value-laden and often closely associated with the normative and interpretive research paradigms presented earlier. You may even come across reference to the terms *quantitative research*, usually taken to mean surveys and experiments, and *qualitative research*, usually taken to mean case study and action research (including practitioner research). It's all a bit fuzzy. Here, the terms *quantitative* and *qualitative* are used simply to refer to types of data (e.g. numbers or words) and the means by which data are analysed and nothing more. Working with numbers can provide a sense of credibility to a study but you may be limited in terms of how far you can go and what you can achieve with them. Working with words can provide a sense of reality to a study but you may be limited in terms of inherent ambiguity and what you can represent.

Working with numbers

In educational research, numbers arise from counting or measuring things in all kinds of different ways. Indeed, whatever your topic, research question or problem, almost anything can be quantified in a numerical sense in one way or another if that's what you want. When considering quantitative data analysis and the use of descriptive statistics, the things that get counted or measured are often referred to as variables. That's because the numbers you arrive at as a result of counting or measuring can vary from one instance to another. Variables can take almost any form and what you call them and how you present them in tabular or graphical form is usually determined by convenience. If this all seems a little abstract, let's develop it further with reference to a hypothetical study of children's television viewing habits with data obtained from only one class in a school using a questionnaire and personal diaries. There are many variables you might be interested in, of course, but let's consider only three.

- TV ownership (data coming from the question *Do you have a television at home?*).

- Personal preference (data coming from responding to the statement *I would rather be inside watching the television at home than outside playing with friends* using a 5-point Likert-type scale).

- Viewing time (data coming from the question *How much time do you spend watching the television on school days at home every week?*).

Do you have a television at home? is a dichotomous question with only two possible answers, yes or no. You either have a television at home or you don't. *TV ownership* is an interesting variable for it is not defined by numbers at all but by words. The responses yes and no are mutually exclusive word categories. The actual numbers of interest come from frequency counting or simply adding up all of the ticks in the yes boxes and all of the ticks in the no boxes provided. Data like this (technically referred to as nominal) could be described in words or presented in a table or a pie chart whichever you think is most appropriate.

I would rather be inside watching television at home than outside playing with friends is a statement which requires a rated response using a Likert-type scale ranging from 1=strongly disagree to 5=strongly agree. The word categories here (strongly disagree to strongly agree) and the numbers chosen to represent them (1 to 5) are ordered and therefore related albeit in an entirely arbitrary way. While the numbers might suggest a regular and equal distance in *strength* of response between categories, it cannot be assumed that this is the case (e.g. you don't know by how much, or in which ways, respondents only agreeing differ from respondents strongly agreeing). Again, the actual numbers of interest for the variable *personal preference* come directly from the scale by frequency counting or adding up all of the circled 1s, 2s, 3s, 4s and 5s (the numbers obtained from using Likert-type scales can be used in many other ways too but this is the simplest level of analysis). Data like this (technically referred to as ordinal) could be described in words or presented in a table or a bar chart whichever you think is most appropriate. It's not impossible to use pie charts but these don't always have the same visual impact.

How much time do you spend watching the television on school days at home every week? is an exact answer question to which any possible amount of time might be provided (well at least on a continuous scale from 0 to 7200 minutes, the total number of minutes available in a 5-day week). The variable *viewing time* is therefore defined by numbers in perhaps a more conventional and familiar form. Any individual viewing time provided would be of little actual use on its own but the average viewing time of the class of children would be worth knowing. Data like this (technically referred to as interval/ratio) could be described in words or presented in a table, a box and whisker plot or a histogram whichever you think is most appropriate.

A problem which commonly arises when dealing with averages is that there is more than one average to consider. The three you are most likely to be familiar with include:

- the mean;

- the median;

- the mode.

The mean is obtained by adding up all of the individual numbers you have in a set of data and dividing the sum by how many actual numbers there are in total. However, the mean is very sensitive to extremely high or low values which can *pull* it up or down accordingly. The median is an average too but an average of a different kind. One way of obtaining the median is to write out all of the numbers you have in a set of data in order from lowest to highest and finding the one that sits right in the middle of them all. The median is not sensitive to extreme values and is often a better average to use than the mean if extremes are present. The mode is also an average but the most inexact. The mode is obtained by looking at each and every number in a set of data and establishing which one occurs most often. Again, if all of this seems a little abstract, let's return to our hypothetical study of children's television viewing habits and the times spent watching television during the week. Imagine these were returned from a small group of 10 children as 75, 75, 75, 75, 105, 105, 150, 210, 450 and 600 minutes. Which average is most representative? You can rule the mode out right away. Despite being the commonest viewing time of four children, 75 minutes is way too low to be of any use. The mean of 192 minutes looks promising but only three children out of the ten watched television longer. It seems to have been affected by some of the more extended viewing times. The median of 105 minutes splits the children into two groups of equal size, five watching for less time and five watching for more. It also seems more aligned with the sample of times as a whole. The median viewing time is perhaps the most representative but it's a tough call between this and the mean. You sometimes need to be able to justify your choice.

Taking the analysis of numbers further requires a more detailed knowledge of mathematics and inferential statistics, the branch of statistics that deals with statistical tests. This is more than we can deal sensibly with here. With computer packages like SPSS, Minitab and even Excel, however, most mathematical manipulations and statistical tests are easy to do and with the minimum of fuss. In the wrong hands, however, it's equally easy to make simple mistakes resulting in completely non-sensical outcomes. If you're not sure about what you're doing and you can't get help, leave it all well alone.

Worked example

Analysing quantitative data

The task

In order to illustrate how to go about analysing numbers using descriptive statistics further we're going to return to three items selected from Jenny's questionnaire first introduced in Chapter 5. You might remember that Jenny was particularly interested in how prepared primary teachers felt to teach across all subject areas of the National Curriculum as well as their recent in-service histories and requirements.

In general, one of the first things Jenny experienced was that things don't always go to plan. Of the 79 questionnaires distributed during the placement briefing, only 55 usable questionnaires were returned, a response rate of 69.6 per cent. Even with a captive audience, the response rate was lower than she'd anticipated. If you're using questionnaires it's important to specify the response rate. This gives away all sorts of information. If the response rate is particularly low, you might begin to wonder about the motivation of those who bothered to fill them in and return them as well as what caused those who didn't to ignore them.

1. Are you male or female?

Appearing as Item 1 (the variable *sex*), Jenny simply counted up the number of male and female boxes ticked and converted frequencies into percentages. She did all of this by hand as it was easy to do. She was then faced with how best to summarise the data. The first thing she did was prepare a word description:

> *Of the 79 questionnaires distributed on the day, 55 usable questionnaires were returned (a response rate of 69.6 per cent). 43 (78.2 per cent) respondents were female and 12 (21.8 per cent) were male.*

But Jenny also knew that she could use a table or a pie chart. At this point she turned to her computer. Preparing a table and a pie chart with straightforward data like this proved relatively easy:

Sex	Frequency (%)
Female	43 (78.2)
Male	12 (21.8)

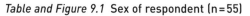

Table and Figure 9.1 Sex of respondent (n=55)

Jenny included everything the reader needed for the table to make sense. The columns and rows were clearly labelled and the sample size was provided alongside the title. The frequencies of male and female respondents were listed from largest to smallest. Percentages, which made comparing the frequencies of males and females easier, were shown in brackets and quoted to one decimal place. Jenny made sure that the frequencies added up to the overall sample size (55 in this case) and that the percentages added up to 100 per cent (rounding errors sometimes mean you only get 99.9 per cent or 100.1 per cent). Jenny applied the same basic principles of presentation to her pie chart. In addition, she included a key in order to identify what the sectors or slices of the pie chart represented. She decided not to add percentages as well as frequencies as the relative sizes of the sectors give these away visually (if in doubt, display both). Jenny used a simple shading to represent the sectors and not bold colours as these were just a distraction. She also chose not to use 3-D and *exploded* sectors as if the pie had been cut as these added nothing to what the pie chart displayed.

Which summary would you choose? It all depends on the importance of the findings and what you're looking to achieve. Within the context of Jenny's work, a simple word description would probably be enough.

2. How prepared do you feel to teach across the curriculum?

Appearing as Item 8 (the variable *preparedness*), Jenny began by working her way through each curriculum area in turn entering data into her computer and using it to count up frequencies and convert them into percentages. She knew straight away that a simple word description of the findings was out of the question. The sheer volume of results was just too great. She also knew that pie charts and bar charts wouldn't work for the same reason (though she did consider using bar charts to compare the differences between specific individual subjects). That left her with a table. Rather than present the table using all twelve areas of the curriculum appearing in their original order, she listed them in order of the subject teachers felt most prepared to teach (English) to the least (music). Even though her computer did all of the hard work for her, she also checked that the frequencies for each and every subject added up to the sample size and every percentage added up to 100 per cent. She introduced and presented the table as follows:

> Overall findings are presented as shown (Table 9.2). One of the most important features to note is the clear difference in perceived preparation to teach across all twelve areas of the National Curriculum from English to music.

3. To what extent do you agree with the following statement?

Appearing as Item 12 (the variable *opportunity*), Jenny continued handling her data in the same way as before. She decided that she could describe the outcome in words but felt that a table, a pie chart or even a bar chart might be better. Once she'd looked at the table and pie chart on her computer she wasn't convinced. The bar chart was visually more appealing and gave a clearer indication of the relative proportions of responses. She introduced and presented the bar chart as follows:

> Overall findings are presented as shown (Figure 9.2). One of the most important features to note is that the teachers were completely divided in their views with almost equal numbers disagreeing as agreeing.

Jenny applied the same basic principles of presentation to her bar chart that she applied to her tables and pie chart. She also remembered to label the axes clearly.

Curriculum area	Very prepared	Sufficiently prepared	Some in-service	Much in-service	Weakest
English	42 (76.4)	11 (20.0)	2 (3.6)	0 (0.0)	0 (0.0)
Mathematics	39 (70.9)	14 (25.4)	2 (3.6)	0 (0.0)	0 (0.0)
Science	36 (65.4)	18 (32.7)	1 (1.8)	0 (0.0)	0 (0.0)
History	29 (52.7)	24 (43.6)	2 (3.6)	0 (0.0)	0 (0.0)
Geography	28 (50.9)	24 (43.6)	3 (5.5)	0 (0.0)	0 (0.0)
PSHE and citizenship	28 (50.9)	21 (38.2)	4 (7.3)	1 (1.8)	1 (1.8)
Religious education	26 (47.3)	21 (38.2)	6 (10.9)	2 (3.6)	0 (0.0)
Physical education	25 (45.4)	21 (38.2)	8 (14.5)	0 (0.0)	1 (1.8)
ICT	22 (40.0)	26 (47.3)	5 (9.1)	2 (3.6)	0 (0.0)
Art and design	20 (36.4)	27 (49.1)	7 (12.7)	0 (0.0)	1 (1.8)
Design and technology	19 (34.5)	26 (47.3)	9 (16.4)	1 (1.8)	0 (0.0)
Music	14 (25.4)	22 (40.0)	11 (20.0)	5 (9.1)	3 (5.5)

Table 9.2 How prepared do you feel to teach across the curriculum? (frequency and percentage; n=55)

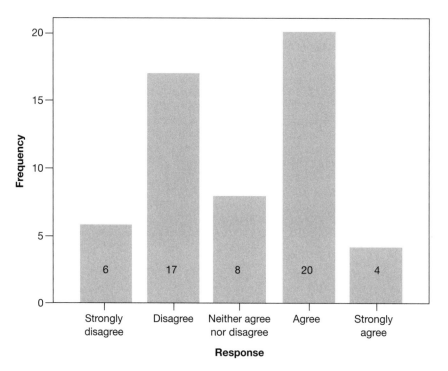

Figure 9.2 In-service opportunity (n=55)

Once again, she decided not to add on percentages. She knew that this was only necessary when comparing data from different groups and when sample sizes varied.

At this point Jenny felt it worth exploring in-service opportunity by the sex of the respondents. Once again, she knew that a simple word description would not be enough so she used her computer to produce a more complicated table and a clustered bar chart:

Sex	Response (frequency and percentage)					
	Strongly disagree	Disagree	Neither agree nor disagree	Agree	Strongly agree	Total
Female	3 (7.0)	11 (25.6)	7 (16.3)	19 (44.2)	3 (7.0)	43 (78.2)
Male	3 (25.0)	6 (50.0)	1 (8.3)	1 (8.3)	1 (8.3)	12 (21.8)
Total	6 (10.9)	17 (30.9)	8 (14.5)	20 (36.4)	4 (7.3)	55 (100.0)

Table 9.3 In-service opportunity (n = 55)

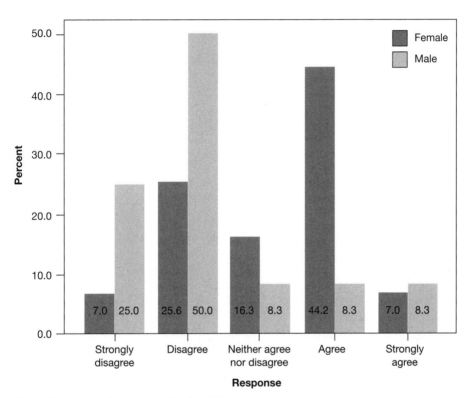

Figure 9.3 In-service opportunity (n = 55)

This time, Jenny's bar chart showed only percentages due to the different number of men and women involved. She summarised this part of her work as follows:

> *On further investigation, the distribution of responses also suggested a split in views between male and female respondents. Men seemed more inclined to feel that in-service opportunity was lacking than women (Table 9.3 or Fig.9.3 – you decide).*

Following a deeper analysis involving an exploration of the relationships between all of the items on her questionnaire, Jenny was eventually left with several options. She could present her findings literally item by item or she could present them in terms of any emergent themes or issues.

Working with words

In educational research, words arise from all kinds of communicative language in all kinds of different ways and content analysis provides a versatile and adaptable means of analysing them. You might also be able to use such alternatives as conversation analysis, discourse analysis and narrative analysis too but these techniques are particularly highly specialised. Content analysis works well for most purposes but especially where text is involved. Categories are the variables of content analysis and these, as determined by convenience, can take almost any form including individual words themselves, key phrases, whole sentences or even entire paragraphs. The steps commonly associated with content analysis are outlined as follows.

- Identify the categories which you think might be of interest to you.

- Establish a coding system which allows the categories to be located within your text with ease.

- Extract and group by category all relevant elements or units of analysis (e.g. the specific words, phrases, sentences or paragraphs themselves).

- Explore in detail all relevant elements or units of analysis within each category group to establish further taxonomic groupings or sub-categories which you think might also be of interest to you.

- Attempt to establish or attribute meaning to findings.

Once again, let's develop all of this further with continued reference to our hypothetical study of children's television viewing habits only this time with data obtained from interview. We'll also retain the same categories of *TV ownership*, *personal preference* and *viewing time*. For the purposes of content analysis, we'll code these quite arbitrarily as *TVO*, *PP* and *VT* respectively. The following interview transcript highlights how the categories of interest are located within the text of the interview using the coding system established (I=interviewer, C=child).

I: Do you have a television at home?
C: Yes. Doesn't everybody? I don't know anybody without a telly. We've got four actually *[EX]*. One in the sitting room, one on the wall in the kitchen and me and my brother's got one in our bedrooms *[TVO]*. He's older than me, he gets to watch it longer *[A]*.
I: Would you rather be inside watching the television at home than outside playing with friends?
C: It depends really. Sometimes if there's something really good on then yeah *[PP]*. There was a really good programme on about the rain forest last night. Did you see it? D'you know, there's more trees and animals in the rain forest than anywhere else on the planet and we're burning it all up *[EX]*. Sad really. I watch other stuff too. Mum let's me watch anything if it'll help with school work. Sometimes we watch it together and talk about it afterwards *[A]*. I enjoy being outside but I'm not allowed out when it rains. Sometimes I watch telly, sometimes I play or read my books *[A]*. I'm not allowed to watch it all the time though. Mum switches it off at nine-o-clock. She says it turns me into a zombie and makes me tired *[A]*.
I: How much time do you spend watching the television on school days at home every week?
C: I've no idea. I'd have to watch it and find out *[VT]*. D'you want me to find out?

You might be wondering by now where the codes *A* for *access* and *EX* for *example* came from. With content analysis, it's sometimes easy to know which categories you might be interested in from the outset. In this particular example, the interview questions themselves make this pretty straightforward. Occasionally, however, other categories come to light only when the text you have is examined closely afterwards as is the case here in our hypothetical example. Pressing on with the analysis to extract and consider the elements or units of analysis associated with *access* gives rise to the following category group.

- He's older than me, he gets to watch it longer. [*age*]

- I watch other stuff too. Mum let's me watch anything if it'll help with school work. Sometimes we watch it together and talk about it afterwards. [*promotion*]

- I enjoy being outside but I'm not allowed out when it rains. Sometimes I watch telly, sometimes I play or read my books. [*alternatives*]

- I'm not allowed to watch it all the time though. Mum switches it off at nine-o-clock. She says it turns me into a zombie and makes me tired. [*restrictions*]

From this one interview transcript alone, at least four additional taxonomic groupings or sub-categories appear to emerge and these have been further labelled on the basis of content as possibly having something to do with *age*, *promotion*, *alternatives* and *restrictions*. From here you can see how content analysis works. Ultimately you'd go through the same process for each category of interest within this one interview transcript and then work your way through all of the interview transcripts you have. By then, some of the factors which appear to influence children's television viewing habits at home will be clear and ready for you to explore in more detail. Content analysis overlaps with descriptive statistics to a degree in that findings may be described in words or taxonomic groupings or sub-categories frequency counted and presented in tabular or graphical form.

The analysis of qualitative data or words can be made easier using computer packages like NUD*IST, Atlas.ti or NVivo. As with quantitative data analysis, however, if you're not sure about what you're doing and you can't get help, leave it all well alone. It's just as easy to use your computer's word processing facility to insert codes and to search for and retrieve the elements or units of analysis you're interested in later.

Worked example

Analysing qualitative data

The task

In order to illustrate how to go about analysing words using content analysis further we're going to return to the worked example of interviewing provided by Warwick introduced in Chapter 6. You might remember that Warwick was particularly interested in the Earth in space. Warwick had hoped to interview 28 Year 6 children but in the end managed only a cross-section of 20. Warwick had already identified the categories which he wished to explore further. One of these was the shape of the Earth itself and we'll pursue this in more detail. The following interview transcript comes from Warwick's own notes and an audio-recording of the interview (R=Researcher – Warwick; C=Cilla aged 11 years 1 month – not her real name):

R: What shape is the Earth?

C: It's round like a ball. A big ball of rock . . . covered in water and clouds.

R: Is there a shape here that's most like the Earth (selection provided)?

C: Yip . . . this one. [Picks up a sphere. Probed: do you know what shapes like that are called?] They're spheres aren't they?

R: How do people know it's that shape?

C: They've gone to the Moon and looked back at it. They did that in 1969. Neil Armstrong was the first man on the Moon . . . he saw it with his own eyes. They've also been out in the Space Shuttle to take pictures of the Earth. If you're in a plane and look out of the window you can see it yourself.

R: Can you draw a picture of what you think the Earth would look like from space? [Draws a circle with land masses including the UK.]

R: What colour would it be?

C: Green and brown, blue and grey for clouds. [Probed: what about the green and brown and blue?] That's the land and seas and oceans.

R: What would you expect to see all around the Earth?

C: Darkness . . . stars and planets . . . the Sun and the Moon.

R: How come we can't see the Earth's 'roundness' when we look out of the window?

C: The Earth's really big.

R: Do you know how big?

C: Is it twelve thousand seven hundred and fifty six kilometres?

R: Have you ever heard of anybody falling off the Earth?

C: No. Well in stories I suppose. They used to think that if you sailed over the horizon you'd come to the edge but there isn't an edge. You'd just keep going 'round until you came back to where you'd started.

R: Could anybody ever fall off the Earth?

C: No . . . it's got gravity. [Probed: what do you mean by gravity?] The Earth's got a pulling force . . . it sort of keeps things from floating off . . . like this . . . [Picks up the sphere selected earlier and lets it drop to the table.]

R: Can you find the Earth in this collection of pictures?

C: That one. [Correct.]

R: What is the Earth?

C: It's a planet.

Warwick decided that the best way to proceed was to transcribe all of the interviews he'd conducted on to one enormous sheet of paper. This allowed him to *see* his data in its entirety and to get a good overall *feel* for what the children had said and done. With only 20 transcripts to work with this didn't present too much of a problem. Using a computer would have been just as easy but he didn't think he'd get as familiar with the data as he needed to be. He then took his lead from the research literature and considered the first *layer* of content analysis to involve establishing just how many correct scientific answers the children provided. This proved a little harder than he thought for the children didn't always provide the textbook responses he'd imagined they would. Nevertheless, he coded his data accordingly and prepared and introduced the following table:

Findings from the first layer of content analysis involving correctness suggest that the children involved in this study already had a reasonably good grasp of many Earth attributes (Table 9.4). In this respect, the overall outcome might be

Interview questions and tasks	Frequency (%)
1. What shape is the earth?	8 (40)
2. Is there a shape here that's most like the Earth (selection provided)?	17 (85)
3. How do people know it's that shape?	12 (60)
4. Can you draw a picture of what you think the Earth would look like from space?	16 (80)
5. What colour would it be?	15 (75)
6. What would you expect to see all around it?	16 (80)
7. How come we can't see the Earth's 'roundness' when we look out of the window?	9 (45)
8. How big is the Earth?	1 (5)
9. Have you ever heard of anybody falling off the Earth?	9 (45)
10. Could anybody ever fall off the Earth?	16 (80)
11. Can you find the Earth in this collection of pictures?	18 (90)
12. What is the Earth?	19 (95)

Table 9.4 Correctness (n = 20)

considered quite positive. The children were, however, almost completely unaware of the Earth's actual size and some found it difficult at times to support their ideas with evidence. Surprisingly, fewer than half of those involved could describe the shape of the Earth accurately using scientific language.

Warwick had noticed as he prepared the table that the number of correct or acceptable verbal descriptions of the Earth's shape was lower than expected. As shape was a category of particular interest in his study he decided to look at this more closely. From the way in which he'd originally organised and managed the data he was quickly able to identify the elements or units of analysis he needed and shift to a second *layer* of content analysis. Frequency counting and tabulating the elements or units of analysis was still the easiest way of facilitating a discussion of what he found:

In response to the question *What shape is the Earth?*, the children interviewed provided one of five responses as indicated (Table 9.5). The most commonly occurring response was round and the least round like a circle. Only about a third of the children used the scientifically more accurate term 'spherical'. This particular finding has very real pedagogical significance in relation to the language teachers use to describe the Earth in classrooms.

Warwick knew in advance of his research that it would be impossible to determine what the children believed the Earth's shape to be from verbal responses to closed

Response	Frequency (%)
Round	8 (40)
Spherical	6 (30)
Round like a ball	2 (10)
Circular	3 (15)
Round like a circle	1 (5)

Table 9.5 What shape is the Earth? (n=20)

questions alone. The only way he could move any further forward was to begin to look in detail at the responses children gave across their individual interviews as a whole. As a consequence, he used content analysis to combine the children's verbal responses with the shapes they selected, how they drew and described the Earth and any other information that would help determine what sorts of models of the Earth the children were carrying around inside their heads. From this, he established that while seventeen children really did think the Earth spherical, two thought it hollow and covered with a dome-like sky and one thought it flat like a pancake. Rather than prepare any more tables, Warwick prepared a series of illustrated *typologies* outlining the basic shape characteristics which defined them. He was then able to compare and contrast these alongside what others had found in the research literature.

When it came to his other categories of interest, the task of making sense of the data proved more and more difficult. With gravity, for example, some of the children's responses were rich and varied and drew attention to a range of errors and misconceptions. A sample of elements or units of analysis are provided as follows:

No . . . it's got gravity . . . The Earth's got a pulling force . . . it sort of keeps things from floating off.

It's got gravity . . . it's like a grip.

Gravity pushes on you like a magnet. You can't fall from the Earth . . . if you set off in one direction you just keep going around and around. It doesn't have an edge to fall from.

You have to live on top of the Earth otherwise you'd fall off.

If you were Warwick, what would you consider doing next? Warwick knew that while it was useful to include quotes and other examples of findings into his final report, it would also be useful to provide at least one example of a full interview transcript too. That way he could begin to demonstrate that his work was relatively free from interviewer effects and the distortion of meaning and misrepresentation. Including a full interview transcript also helped make the point that as well as investigating children's ideas, he was also interested in their thoughts and reasoning.

Summary of key points

Always consult the research literature to see how others have tackled the issue of data analysis. It might save you a lot of time and unnecessary anxiety.

Don't worry if you can't always identify the five stages of data analysis. They're not always readily apparent.

The terms quantitative and qualitative mean different things to different people. Don't get bogged down in the philosophy of it all. It's probably not worth it.

There's no need to be afraid of numbers. You just need to know how to handle them. Keep everything simple and you'll be fine.

Content analysis may sometimes feel like taking a long road for a shortcut. So take as many shortcuts as you like. As long as you outline what you are doing and why you'll be fine.

Further reading

Almost every research methods textbook contains advice on analysing data but those by Gellman (1973) on numbers and Bogdan and Biklen (1992) and Miles and Huberman (1994) on words are classics. Connolly (2007) covers descriptive and inferential statistics for the beginner particularly well while Field (2005) is only for those with a more detailed knowledge of all statistics and the computer package SPSS. Silverman (2000) and Mason (2002) are also worth consulting.

Bogdan, R.G. and Biklen, S.K. (1992) *Qualitative research for education.* Boston: Allyn and Bacon.

Coffey, A. and Atkinson, P. (1996) *Making sense of qualitative data: complementary strategies.* London: Sage.

Connolly, P. (2007) *Quantitative data analysis in education: a critical introduction using SPSS.* London: Routledge.

Field, A. (2005) *Discovering statistics using SPSS.* London: Sage.

Gellman, E.S. (1973) *Descriptive statistics for teachers.* New York: Harper and Row.

Gibbs, G. (2006) *How to analyse qualitative data.* London: Sage.

Mason, J. (2002) *Qualitative researching.* London: Sage.

Miles, M.L. and Huberman, A.M. (1994) *Qualitative data analysis: an expanded sourcebook.* London: Sage.

Silverman, D. (2000) *Doing qualitative research: a practical handbook.* London: Sage.

10. Writing up

Learning outcomes

Writing up brings with it a great sense of relief. The end is very much in sight. But writing up also involves conventions, word limits and deadlines. By having read this chapter and completed the tasks within it, you will:

- know about submitting your individual research project as a formal piece of academic writing;

- be aware of some of the common mistakes involved in writing up and how to avoid them;

- be able to identify plagiarism and what it means to plagiarise the work of others.

Don't spoil it now

As you eventually move towards the completion of your individual research project don't forget to stop and think about how far you've come. By this point, you'll have read what you could in the time available, settled on a topic worthy of investigation, gone *out there* and collected data, and nearly finished analysing it all. With the end in sight, however, this is where it can all go wrong. All that effort counts for nothing if what you write up is not up to scratch. When it's finally ready and submitted, your individual research project will be treated first and foremost as a formal piece of academic writing based entirely on the research activity planned and undertaken by you. Writing up in this way is as much an art form as it is an acquired skill and nowhere near as straightforward as it sounds. Even fast writers only manage to draft between 500 and 1000 words a day, for example, so leave as much time for writing up as you can. Be prepared to also proof read and edit several versions before it ever starts to *look* and *feel* right.

Structure

One of the first things to consider when writing up is structure. A *typical* individual research project normally includes the following sections:

- title page;

- abstract;

- list of contents;

- introduction (Chapter 1);

- review of literature (Chapter 2);

- outline of methodology (Chapter 3);

- presentation and analysis of findings (Chapter 4);

- conclusions and implications (Chapter 5);

- reference list;

- appendices.

Individual research projects are structured like this in order for you to demonstrate that you can write clearly and coherently at an appropriate level for your intended audience, to outline your contribution to the field of knowledge in a standardised way and because what you submit gets marked or graded and you have no choice! The truth is, you can include as many or as few sections as you need and call them whatever you like. Here, we're simply following convention. So unless directed otherwise, you are advised to do the same. It would be quite wrong to conclude from the list of sections outlined here, however, that you should wait until the last moment and write everything up from beginning to end in one go. Instead, you should try to write up your individual research project as the work itself proceeds, starting with the review of literature which is often the first thing you do. It's hard, for example, to write an abstract or even an introduction before you know how the research will unfold or what you'll find. Don't assume your reader will not be interested in the abstract or introduction though. These sections will be read first even if written last and it's important to create the right impression from the beginning. It's increasingly common to find acknowledgements inserted towards the start of individual research projects too and in many instances acknowledgements can be important. But this not the place to thank your parents for bringing you into the world and helping you to become the person you are or to thank your pets for their patience and undivided attention.

After structure, you're most likely going to want to know how many words you should allocate to each section. There is no easy answer to this, of course, but as a general rule of thumb, devote about one half of your word limit to the introduction, review of literature and methodology and the other half to the presentation and analysis of findings and conclusions and implications. Each individual research project is pretty much unique and only you can determine how words should be allocated further. Do check what counts towards your word limit carefully. Abstracts, lists of contents, tables, charts, graphs and other illustrations, references and appendices are usually excluded. If this is the case, consider how to use them wisely. Do not exceed your word limit under any circumstances. If you do, your work will almost certainly be penalised. That said, always begin by writing what you *need* to write. This is important no matter how many words it takes initially. It's a whole lot easier to edit out and down than to make up later. In any case, editing through several drafts usually helps turn a fairly *immature* individual research project into a great one. Each section of a *typical* individual research project is presented in more detail as follows.

Title page

The title page should include, in order, at least the name of your institution, the title of your individual research project, your own name, the title of your course (with specific course codes if applicable) and the date of submission. The title of your project, now firmly developed from the working title you came up with earlier, should accurately reflect the nature and content of your work. Subtitles are on the increase but should only be used where absolutely necessary. The title (with or without a subtitle) should be kept as short as possible and not normally exceed two lines in length. It's easy when looking for a title to allow everything to get longer and longer and longer. Don't let this happen! The title page usually also doubles as the front cover. Pictures should only be added to title pages if they make some meaningful contribution and not for decoration.

Abstract

The abstract is an important source of information intended to capture the interest and attention of the reader and *draw* them in. You should already know how valuable abstracts can be from your own review of literature. Your own abstract should present a summary of your individual research project as a whole and the importance or noteworthiness of findings in only a few well chosen words. Aim for about 250 or so. The only way to become a good abstract writer is to read as many different abstracts as you can and study their characteristics closely. When it comes to writing your own, just don't be vague.

List of contents

The list of contents is just that! It's a list showing all of the sections of your individual research project alongside the page numbers you'd expect to find them starting on. It's common to only start numbering pages from the introduction and not the abstract or list of contents itself. If you've used subheadings within sections to help improve the structure of your work, these may be added into the list of contents too. A separate list of tables, charts, graphs and other illustrations can be useful. Always present your list of contents neatly and in tabular form.

Introduction

The introduction should provide sufficient background information to help contextualise your work for the reader as well as to help *ease* them into the detail which follows. As such, you need to say something about your choice of topic and what you hoped to achieve by way of investigating it. This may require you to state your research question or to outline the nature of the problem you were looking to solve. You should certainly draw attention to where the research took place and who was involved. It may be worth pointing out here that your work is small-scale and to highlight some of the strengths and limitations associated with this. Don't slip into writing informally just because it's the introduction.

Review of literature

The literature review should demonstrate that you as the researcher are familiar with *the field* surrounding your chosen topic. The only way to achieve this is by drawing upon and summarising the information contained within an appropriate balance of credible academic sources including journal articles, textbooks and websites. The literature review can also be a useful place for you to provide the definitions and meanings attached to specific technical terms which the reader may not be familiar with and which you need to use frequently (sometimes definitions and meanings appear in the introduction, it's a matter of *flow* and personal choice). It's easy when preparing a literature review to write descriptively rather than critically. You need to remember to do both. It's also easy when replicating an existing study to forget to bring everything up to date. Try to bring your literature review to a close by outlining clearly where your own work *fits in*.

Methodology

Methodology concerns itself with every step and procedure involved in carrying out a piece of research. Within the methodology section, you should attempt to describe and justify not only how you went about addressing your research question or solving your problem but why you went about it that way. In essence, this gives away something of your own values and beliefs as a researcher (implicitly or explicitly). You need to provide a complete and detailed account of the location and participants involved and how you came to be in that location with those participants in the first place (e.g. access and sampling). You need to provide a complete and detailed account of how your research tools were obtained or constructed, their strengths and limitations, and the extent to which your data might be considered valid and reliable. You also need to provide a complete and detailed account of any ethical matters arising as a result of your work and what action you took to address them. You might begin to get concerned by this point that some of the write up is becoming a bit repetitive with similar information already appearing in the abstract and introduction. Just try to remember that section by section you're *easing* your reader further and further into your work and adjust what you've written accordingly. If replicating an existing study, don't forget to point out the similarities and differences involved.

Presentation and analysis of findings

So what did you find out and was it worthwhile? Sometimes it's entirely appropriate to consider the presentation and analysis of findings together; sometimes it's entirely appropriate to keep the presentation and analysis of findings apart. You'll probably be led by the nature of the findings themselves and know what to do almost intuitively. Try to include tables, charts, graphs and other illustrations where possible. These not only help to summarise data effectively, they can help lift the general appearance of your work as well as save words. It's here that you should attempt to demonstrate your ability to raise and sustain an argument in support of any position adopted. One of the hardest things you'll ever have to do when writing up this section is to determine what stays and what goes. Unless your word limit is particularly generous, you just won't be able to fit in everything you want to. Some of the data you worked so hard to get will almost certainly get left behind. This is common and not something you should worry about. Don't forget to end the section by telling the reader how your findings sit alongside the body of research literature already available and which you have reviewed.

Conclusions and implications

Your individual research project should come to an end with an overall summary of everything you did and everything you found. This usually involves returning to your research question or problem once again in order to evaluate and reflect upon how successful or not your work has been. It's also important to give careful consideration to what implications your findings might have in relation to *the field* surrounding your chosen topic (e.g. theoretical, practical, pedagogical, organisational). As with the presentation and analysis of findings, sometimes it's easier to write the conclusions and implications together and sometimes it's better to keep them apart. Ensure that your conclusions are consistent with your findings and don't over-generalise beyond the boundaries and limitations of the research itself. It's quite easy to think that you can get away with neglecting this section and save words because it only summarises what's already been presented in the main body of text. Think otherwise.

Reference list

The reference list should contain full details of only the research literature actually referred to or cited in each and every section of your work. Unless directed otherwise, the reference list should be constructed in accordance with the Harvard System (author-date) with all source materials appearing in alphabetical order. It's often acceptable to present journal articles, textbooks and websites in separate lists but this is not necessary at all. Don't confuse a reference list with a bibliography. A bibliography usually contains details of a wider range of source materials including items which you may have consulted during your work and found interesting but never found occasion to use.

Appendices

Appendices should be used sparingly. Indeed, it should be possible to prepare an individual research project without using a single appendix at all. If you must include appendices, however, use them with care. A *typical* appendix might include, for example, a blank copy of the research tool you used such as a questionnaire, but not the entire collection of questionnaires that were completed and returned. Similarly, an appendix is not the place to cram in every piece of children's work you collected during a placement. Appendices have a tendency to become the *dustbins* of individual research projects, containing anything and everything that can't squeeze into the main body of text. That's not what they're for.

Worked example

Writing up a research project

The task

There is no one formula for writing up an individual research project though it is possible to standardise structure, writing style and general presentation to a degree. Here, we return to the work of Rebecca whose research proposal was introduced earlier in Chapter 2. Edited highlights from the abstract and five main sections of what she eventually submitted are used to illustrate a few of the finer points of writing up. Don't be put off by the subject matter. That's not what's important here. Concentrate instead on the *story* which is still very much evident. Compare what you read below alongside her original research proposal to get an idea of how far things moved on in the time available.

1. Revised title

The vocabulary of Key Stage 2 mathematics

[Rebecca changed the title of her project to this to more accurately reflect her work.]

2. Abstract

Constructed upon a highly specialised and technical vocabulary, mathematics is rendered futile without words. Despite recognition and a high profile within national educational policy, research into children's knowledge, understanding and use of mathematical vocabulary remains something of a void within contemporary educational research. Based primarily upon the questionnaire methodologies of investigations carried out in the 1970s, supplemented with unstructured group interviews and non-participant observation, this study attempts to make a valuable contribution in this area by exploring the mathematical vocabulary held by 50 Year 6 pupils in two closely located primary schools. Despite encouraging levels of familiarity with 15 mathematical terms considered important enough to be included within the National Numeracy Strategy and introduced by the end of Key Stage 2, an abundance of errors and misconceptions were displayed by all participants. The development of children's mathematical vocabulary is therefore identified as a cause for concern. In light of the findings, it is suggested that greater emphasis be placed upon the identification and resolution of semantic mathematical difficulties if a secure foundation in numeracy and mathematics is ever to be achieved.

[Rebecca's abstract is well constructed and conveys an accurate account of her project as a whole, all in under 200 words. It's presented in italics to distinguish it from the main body of text which follows. It's also written mainly in the present tense. Most abstracts are but can you think why?]

3. Introduction

. . . The following task, taken from a Key Stage 2 mathematics test paper, provides a standard example of the mathematical problems children face every day:

Shade in two squares to make a symmetrical pattern.

Within this single example, the mathematical words *square* and *symmetry* play a central role. For an individual *fluent* in mathematics, the meaning of the task is clear. With no knowledge of vocabulary or the language of mathematics, it would be impossible for a child to even attempt to begin or to advance their mathematical understanding.

[In addition to everything else, Rebecca placed this published task within the introduction to illustrate the importance of mathematical vocabulary and language. Contextualised in this way, the reader is left in no doubt as to the nature of the problem as she saw it.]

4. Review of literature

. . . The educational issue surrounding vocabulary, although only recently reaching the forefront of government initiatives in mathematics, is far from new. . . . Despite providing deep insight into the field, however, the works of Otterburn and Nicholson (1976) and Nicholson (1977) share two significant limitations. Firstly, their samples included only secondary school pupils. Secondly, the studies were conducted before the introduction of the National Curriculum and National Numeracy Strategy and the changes these initiatives brought with them to mathematics education. . . . While the research of both Mayow (2000) and Raiker (2002) is more up-to-date and includes children in the primary sector, these studies have their limitations too. In contrast to the quantitative data collected in the 1970s, both relied on subjective observations of unspecified registers of terminology and the more qualitative approach arguably lacked the rigour provided earlier.

[After extensive review, Rebecca began to concentrate on the research presented in four key articles. More importantly, she began to compare and contrast the research and develop a critique of the field in terms of its limitations.]

5. Methodology

. . . In light of the pioneering approach of Otterburn and Nicholson (1976) and Nicholson (1977), the questionnaire used here presented the children involved with a list of mathematical terms. For each term, the participants were required to respond to two questions in particular: *Do I know this word?* and *Do I understand this word?* By then taking this further in the style of Mayow (2000) and Raiker (2002) and asking the children to expand upon their responses by drawing and describing what each term meant to them later, their levels of semantic understanding could be more accurately and reliably determined. Remaining within the approach introduced by these authors, the children's responses could be placed into one of three categories.

- Correct – the child understood what the term meant.

- Confused – the child confused the word with another or displayed an error or misunderstanding.

- Blank – the child made no attempt to describe the term at all.

[Rebecca signalled and justified here that she was adopting a mixed-method approach based upon her reading of the literature and then went on to show how the children's responses would be categorised. Her acknowledgement of earlier work helps avoid any charge of plagiarism.]

6. Presentation and analysis of findings

Mathematical term	Year of introduction	Do I know this word?	Do I under-stand this word?	Evidence-based level of semantic understanding		
		Yes	Yes	Blank	Confused	Correct
Square	Reception	50 (100)	50 (100)	0 (0)	0 (0)	50 (100)
Cube	Reception	50 (100)	49 (98)	0 (0)	0 (0)	50 (100)
Sphere	Reception	50 (100)	50 (100)	0 (0)	4 (8)	46 (92)
Cuboid	Year 1	50 (100)	50 (100)	1 (2)	7 (14)	42 (84)
Hexagon	Year 2	50 (100)	49 (98)	0 (0)	10 (20)	40 (80)
Pentagon	Year 2	50 (100)	47 (94)	3 (6)	13 (26)	34 (68)
Quadrilateral	Year 3	46 (92)	37 (74)	11 (22)	8 (16)	31 (62)
Perimeter	Year 4	46 (92)	41 (82)	11 (22)	12 (24)	27 (54)
Rectangle	Reception	49 (98)	48 (96)	2 (4)	33 (66)	15 (30)
Polygon	Year 4	40 (80)	15 (30)	37 (74)	8 (16)	5 (10)
Radius	Year 4	24 (48)	14 (28)	33 (66)	13 (26)	4 (8)
Oblong	Year 4	35 (70)	13 (26)	34 (68)	14 (28)	2 (4)
Diameter	Year 4	31 (62)	12 (24)	37 (74)	12 (24)	1 (2)
Perpendicular	Year 4	26 (52)	7 (14)	40 (80)	9 (18)	1 (2)
Congruent	Year 5	10 (20)	0 (0)	49 (98)	1 (2)	0 (0)

Table 10.1 **Children's knowledge, understanding and use of mathematical vocabulary by the end of Key Stage 2 (frequency and percentage; n = 50)**

[Rebecca presented her findings as expected. In the first of several tables, however, she gives the reader a summary of outcomes which she argued with other findings that her initial concerns were justified. There could be many reasons for this, of course, and these she teased out in detail.]

7. Conclusions and implications

... Based upon the methodologies of previous authors, evidence was provided to suggest predominantly high levels of familiarity with certain mathematical terms. In agreement with Mayow (2000) and Raiker (2002), however, familiarity did not always extend to understanding and errors and misconceptions among those children participating in this study remained common. ... Though drawn from only a small sample of children in two primary schools, the disturbing significance of these findings, which echo the outcomes obtained in studies conducted by Otterburn and Nicholson (1976) and Nicholson (1977) with older pupils over 30 years ago, becomes vivid in the consideration of their classroom implications and the impact of the National Curriculum and National Numeracy Strategy.

[Among her many conclusions and discussion of implications, Rebecca considered her own findings in relation to the work of others.]

Writing style

For an individual research project to be submitted as a formal piece of academic writing you have to adopt a writing style to suit. The two most common styles in use today focus either on the content and findings of the research itself (the content-oriented style) or the process leading to its completion (the process-oriented style). The characteristics of each style are very different. Content-oriented writing reports research in the third person and often at a discrete personal distance (e.g. 15 questionnaires were distributed among the teachers of the placement school). Process-oriented writing reports research in the first person and often as a journey of self-discovery (e.g. I felt it necessary to distribute 15 questionnaires to each and every teacher within my placement school). These two styles betray a striking alignment with the normative and interpretive research paradigms as well as some of the research approaches presented earlier. Indeed, focusing on content and findings is often considered best suited to surveys and experiments while focusing on process is often considered best suited to case studies and action research (including practitioner research). Like all attempts to classify or categorise things in education, however, nothing is ever that straightforward. So once again, we're going to stick with convention. Unless directed otherwise, adopt the style which focuses on content and findings. There are actually several good reasons for this.

- It's the most commonly adopted style by a long way and the one you've probably encountered most often yourself.

- It's generally most *fit-for-purpose* and covers all eventualities (including writing up most case studies and action or practitioner research).

- It's the easier of the two to adopt and use well.

Formal process-oriented writing is more difficult than it might appear at first sight and when studying education or training to be a teacher for the first time you need to keep risk avoidance high on your list of priorities.

Reflective task

Content vs process

The characteristic features of content-oriented and process-oriented writing are very different.

- Content-oriented – written in the third person, past tense and passive voice, presented at a discrete personal distance, objective, realist and summative in nature.

- Process-oriented – written in the first person, present tense and active voice, presented as a journey of self-discovery, subjective, confessionalist and formative in nature.

Consider what the characteristic features of each style might look like within the context of writing up your own individual research project. To what extent do you think that the characteristic features of each style are mutually exclusive? Despite suggesting that you persevere with a content-oriented style as a matter of sticking with convention, and thereby allowing the reader to focus more on what is being said than who is saying it, it's perfectly possible to write formally adopting a process-oriented style too. It just takes more care and thought. Obtain a copy of the following article (print or online):

- Pennycook, A. (1994) The politics of pronouns. *ELT Journal*, 48(2): 173–178.

This article points out in no uncertain terms that writing style is far more important than you might imagine. It's all about ownership, voice, power and representation. Should writing really be that political?

Overall presentation

In addition to adopting a content-oriented style, you should also think very carefully about other aspects of overall presentation too. A short list of points to consider might include the following.

- Write in the past tense as well as in the third person.

- Word-process your project using a sensible font, font size and line spacing (a 12-point Arial or Times New Roman font with a line spacing of 1.5 looks particularly good).

- Adjust the left and right margins to allow a slightly larger gap on the left for stapling or binding.

- Insert page numbers at the bottom of each page from the introduction on and remember to change the page number default setting to your chosen text font.

- Try not to insert headers and footers or use footnotes and endnotes.

- Separate paragraphs by inserting a single line space between them (over-paragraphing work is a growing *disease* so try not to).

- Anonymise *real people* in *real settings* by giving them relevant if fictitious names rather than referring to them as Child 1 and Location X.

- When using tables, charts, graphs and other illustrations, avoid bold colours, remember to label all of the axes or other components where necessary, give everything a title, size each and every one to occupy no more than about half a page, and make sure you actually refer to everything within the main body of text (the same applies to appendices).

It's important to try to remember that a good individual research project tells a good *story* too. The *story* should be sufficiently transparent and easy to follow that the reader doesn't have to ask any difficult and penetrating questions. You can try to improve the quality of your *story* in the following ways.

- By ensuring that you link each section of the project together (e.g. *The purpose of this chapter is . . .* , *As we shall see in the next chapter . . .*).

- By signalling that you are aware of the uncertainty sometimes attached to adopting a position (e.g. *Here, it could be argued . . .* , *Within the limitations of the methodology . . .* , *By interpreting the findings in this way . . .* , *It might be concluded from this . . .*).

- By using less direct language (e.g. *perhaps . . .* , *it would appear that . . .* , *possibly . . .* , *this would suggest . . .* , *it might be . . .*).

- By using language which indicates support for or an extension of ideas, views and opinions (*similarly . . .* , *equally . . .* , *likewise . . .* , *furthermore . . .* , *in addition . . .*).

- By using language which indicates an opposition of ideas, views and opinions (*alternatively . . .* , *on the other hand . . .* , *conversely . . .* , *that said . . .*).

Aim for nothing short of the highest standard of grammar, spelling and punctuation throughout and do not under any circumstances rely solely on the spelling and grammar checkers found on your computer as these are by no means foolproof. Have a critical friend read your work thoroughly and take any criticisms they offer on the chin. This strategy relies on your critical friend being sufficiently literate to comment and sufficiently confident to tell you if they find anything you need to change. Obtain feedback on the structure and presentation of your work, including your writing style, from your supervisor as soon as possible. When you do come to hand it all in, make sure that all of the pages are present and in the right order and that if it's a copy that everything is straight on the page. Remember, the ultimate responsibility for writing up rests with you.

Practical task

Spot the mistakes

When your work is read, a high standard of literacy will be expected throughout. Literacy may even appear as a marking or grading criterion. Rewrite the passage of text below correcting all of the common mistakes in grammar, spelling and punctuation you can find. Consider finding 20 something of a benchmark. If you can't find at least that many you might wish to seek out some help.

> *It was some time ago in the late 1990's that I decided to give up my job and change career. I'd moved into marketing after graduating and really found myself in a bit of a rut. My principle reason for choosing teaching revolved around the holidays. Well that and the pay. No, seriously, I'm only joking. As the mother of two small children I'd been into school so many times I'd started to feel very much at home there. I wanted to turn what was virtually a past-time into a passion. All of my friends and family thought I was daft, of course, as teaching didn't seem to command the same status as my previous line of work.*

Practical task continued

On being offered a place at my first choice institution, however, I lept at the opportunity. My pre-course placement was fantastic and confirmed for me that my committment to becoming a member of the teaching proffesion was not misplaced. I felt really priviliged to be there and the staff made every effort to accomodate me and put up with my total lack of experience. I never felt akward being there once. I came away with a real sense that despite all of the regulation and exagerated bad press you really did have a lot of autonomy and independance. I guess there right when they say you should never beleive what you hear on the news and read in the papers. The thing about teaching is that you just never know what tommorow will bring. Teaching is'nt anything like the day to day monotany of trying to sell stuff to people who dont want to buy it. After other trips into school including the opportunity to work with paralell year groups in key stage one and seperate Year 5 and 6 classes in Key stage 2 I aquired more confidence and expertise. I became more skillful at planning and delivering lessons. The course work was grate too and I past everything first time. It was my dream come true. You really can have an affect on childrens' lives. I've never looked back really and I'd definately never go back. I love it.

The passage itself was obtained from a teacher's autobiographical account of how they came to enter the profession. In this case, the mistakes were added in for effect. Just imagine for a moment how you'd feel if you were given an entire project littered with mistakes like this to read. How would you mark or grade it?

Plagiarism

Plagiarism is a form of cheating and a serious academic offence. Fortunately, it's still quite rare. Thanks mainly to the internet, however, cases of plagiarism are rather sadly on the increase. Plagiarism occurs when you present somebody else's work as your own without proper acknowledgement. While most cases of plagiarism centre around the copying of entire chunks of text, individual sentences, phrases or even specific words, plagiarism can also involve the borrowing of other people's ideas, views and opinions. There are basically two types of plagiarism, which are:

- intentional;

- unintentional.

Both are unacceptable and there is no defence for either. Short of deliberately setting out to cheat, most cases of plagiarism, intentional or unintentional, can be ascribed to poor study and research skills and the coping strategies adopted when stressed and running out of time. The penalties for plagiarism can be quite severe and usually depend upon the extent to which you have plagiarised, whether or not you are a repeat offender and how you respond when challenged. In order to write up your individual research project you need to be able summarise the work of others of course. But you can't just cut and paste freely from one document into another or paraphrase without at least attempting to change things into your own words or word swap using a thesaurus and hope to get away with it. Plagiarism is remarkably easy to detect so just don't do it.

Spotting plagiarism

Read the following passage of text carefully. It was extracted with slight modification from Hewitt, R. and Hopkins, E. (2006) Polarisations in English. In: J. Sharp, S. Ward and L. Hankin (eds) *Education Studies: an issues-based approach.* Exeter: Learning Matters. 75–82.

> *Considering the fact that English is no real newcomer to the school curriculum, it is quite remarkable that it has been an almost constant subject of controversy and debate. Strong views and polarisations have characterised the history of English teaching that continue to the present day. It has been argued, for example, that even as recently as the 1980s, English teaching concentrated too much on personal responses and creativity to the detriment of other things more formal. The fact that English teaching experienced a massive shift back towards formality with the introduction of a National Literacy Strategy in the 1990s is typical of the pendulum-like nature of developments in English in schools.*

Now read the four summaries of the same text below. These represent the sorts of summaries which often appear in individual research projects. Would you describe any of them as fully plagiarised or do any of them contain sufficient evidence which might lead you to conclude that they're at least partially plagiarised? Are any of them plagiarism free? How would you describe the form of plagiarism (e.g. cut and paste, paraphrase or word swap)? During your deliberations, consider what is also referred to as *common knowledge*. Some information is just so common-place that there is no longer any need to trace it back to its original source or to acknowledge the original author (assuming there ever was one). Establishing what counts as *common knowledge* can be tricky to say the least. Do any of the summaries contain any evidence of what you might regard as *common knowledge*?

> *Considering the fact that English is no real newcomer to the school curriculum, it is quite remarkable that it has been an almost constant subject of controversy and debate. Strong views and polarisations have characterised the history of English teaching that continue to the present day (Hewitt and Hopkins, 2006, p. 75). The replacement of a personalised and creative approach to English teaching with a National Literacy Strategy in schools in England and Wales in the 1990s exemplifies the pendulum-like swing of opposing views.*

> *According to Hewitt and Hopkins (2006), English teaching in schools in England and Wales has been strongly influenced by both liberalist and*

Practical task continued

traditionalist ideologies and perspectives which have alternated periodically with the passage of time.

As no real newcomer to the school curriculum in England and Wales, English remains the subject of continued controversy and debate. The pendulum-like nature of developments in English teaching has been evident from even as recently as the 1980s, when the dominant ideology supported a more personal and creative approach, to the 1990s, when the dominant ideology supported a return to formality and prescription.

English has always been a part of the school curriculum in England and Wales. But strong views over expectation in terms of outcome as a result of English teaching have remained somewhat polarised with pendulum-like swings from a focus on personal responses and creativity to a more structured approach including that, perhaps, of the National Literacy Strategy (Hewitt and Hopkins, 2006).

Summary of key points

Make sure you plan to leave as much time to write up as you possibly can. It'll take a whole lot longer than you think it will. Poor write ups usually attract poor marks or low grades.

Check that you've presented your work in accordance with the guidelines presented here or in your own course handbook, whichever takes priority. This extends to observing conventions, remaining within word limits and submitting on time.

If you find that what you're writing is becoming a little repetitive, adjust the detail in each section accordingly.

Use tables, charts, graphs and other illustrations to summarise and improve the overall appearance of your work and to save words.

Don't squeeze every last piece of data you collect into appendix after appendix. This isn't what they're for.

Experiment with fonts, font sizes, line spacing and any other aspects of presentation you like. Just remember that what you think looks good may not be appropriate for this sort of work at all.

Try to write up clearly, coherently, convincingly and persuasively. Imagine you are telling a story. It all has to join up and flow.

Ensure the highest standards of grammar, spelling and punctuation throughout. If you need help then seek it out.

Acknowledge your sources at all time and take care not to plagiarise the work of others even when summarising and paraphrasing.

Further reading

Almost every research methods textbook contains advice on writing up but Cottrell (2003) offers particularly valuable practical support. If your own grammar, spelling and punctuation need some work, there's no better self-help source than Wyse (2007).

Cottrell, S. (2003) *The study skills handbook*. London: Palgrave.

Wyse, D. (2007) *The good writing guide for education students*. London: Sage.

Index